Queer Disability

The Queer and Disabled Movements through their Personalities

Daisy Holder

First published in Great Britain in 2024 by
Pen & Sword History
An imprint of
Pen & Sword Books Ltd
Yorkshire – Philadelphia
Copyright © Daisy Holder 2024
ISBN 9781399050579

The right of Daisy Holder to be identified as Author of this work has been asserted by them in accordance with the Copyright, Designs and Patents Act 1988.

A CIP catalogue record for this book is available from the British Library.

All rights reserved. No part of this book may be reproduced or transmitted in any form or by any means, electronic or mechanical including photocopying, recording or by any information storage and retrieval system, without permission from the Publisher in writing.

Set in Aldine 401 13/16.75
Printed and bound in the UK by CPI Group (UK) Ltd., Croydon. CR0 4YY

Pen & Sword Books Limited incorporates the imprints of After the Battle, Archaeology, Atlas, Aviation, Battleground, Discovery, Family History, History, Maritime, Military, Politics, Select, Transport, True Crime, Fiction, Frontline Books, Leo Cooper, Praetorian Press, Seaforth Publishing, Wharncliffe and White Owl.

For a complete list of Pen & Sword titles please contact
PEN & SWORD BOOKS LIMITED
George House, Beevor Street, Off Pontefract Road, Hoyle Mill, Barnsley, South Yorkshire, England, S71 1HN
E-mail: enquiries@pen-and-sword.co.uk
Website: www.pen-and-sword.co.uk
Or
PEN AND SWORD BOOKS
1950 Lawrence Rd, Havertown, PA 19083, USA
E-mail: Uspen-and-sword@casematepublishers.com
Website: www.penandswordbooks.com

Alex, thanks for washing the dishes so many times while I was busy writing this.

Contents

A Note on Language	9
Frida Kahlo: 'The main character in her own mythology' *The Social Model of Disability / Shared Queer and Disability History*	11
Marsha P. Johnson: 'The fairies were not supposed to riot' *The Stonewall Riots / HIV and AIDS Activism*	24
Kitty Cone: 'Their goals were unfeasible and their lifestyles improper' *The 504 Sit In / The Americans with Disabilities Act*	40
Connie Panzarino: 'Trached dykes eat pussy without coming up for air' *Working While Disabled / Healthcare Discrimination / Disability Pride*	66
Sharon Kowalski & Karen Thompson: 'Sharon chose her family, but the judge didn't agree.' *Guardianship / Family of Affinity*	80
Lord Byron: 'Such a strange melange of good and evil' *Queerness in 18th and 19th Century / The Crime of Homosexuality*	98
Alan Turing: 'A rather painful interest for a young man' *Turing's Law / Decriminalisation of Homosexuality*	117
Barbara Jordan: 'As cozy as a piledriver' *Employment Rights for LGBTQ+ / Disability Rights before the ADA*	134
Dr John Fryer: 'You may take this as a declaration of war' *Queerness in the Diagnostic and Statistical Manual / Homosexuality as Mental Illness*	153
Harriet Martineau: 'Frightened on beholding the human face' *Hypnosis / Conversion Therapy*	169
Bobbie Lea Bennet: 'None of us are looking to make this thing sensational' *Medicare / Gender Identity Clinics*	192

Michelangelo: 'Weep, you girls, my penis has given you up'   213
Disabled Poetry / Homoerotic Poetry

Acknowledgements   232
Bibliography   233
Index   240

A Note on Language

This book features several historical terms for disability which would now be considered offensive. It also features several historical terms to refer to LGBTQ+ people, which would now be considered very offensive. After many years of research, I'm relatively immune to it, but for those not expecting it, it can be a shock. I choose to refer to 'the Disabled community' and 'the Queer community', as these are the terms I use for myself and my peers, and those they use for me. I use the word Disabled to mean anyone with a long-term impairment that affects their ability to do daily activities or interact with the world. As a result, I include physical impairments, chronic illnesses, sensory impairments, neurodivergence, learning disabilities and mental health conditions within this bracket, although it is up to an individual to identify as Disabled and therefore not everyone who may be within those brackets will see themselves as Disabled. I use LGBTQ+ in this book. While I include asexual and intersex people within the community of Queer, and they are welcome within our family, those groups have not featured in my research. In consultation with Ace and Intersex pals, I have decided to use this shorter acronym for that reason. As I am in Britain, I use British English spelling unless it is the name of a place (hence you'll probably see a Center followed closely by a centre). Similarly, not only do we not use the terms handicapped, handicapable, differently-abled, people of determination, disAbled or diversability, but if you try to use them in my community there is a good chance that someone will assault you.

Frida Kahlo

'The main character in her own mythology'

There are very few people in the world today who wouldn't recognise the image of Frida Kahlo. Even if they don't know her name, or remember her art, they recognise the monobrowed woman whose face adorns clothing, homeware, countless books, and films about her life. In fact, her silhouette has become so ubiquitous that while I was writing this introduction, a chair was abandoned outside my block of flats with multiple versions of her face on the seat.

While she was both bisexual and Disabled, it is incredibly rare to find an article or account of her life of any kind that examines both things together. Writers will take apart the different sections of her identity and examine them one at a time, without really considering how they worked together to alter her life experience. The habit of compartmentalising someone's life into easily digestible chunks does a disservice to the many of us who are both Queer and Disabled, and contributes to the misunderstandings about each community in the other. Part of this is due to how much more common disability is among Queer individuals. According to research from 2022, disability is 156 per cent more prevalent among LGBTQ+ people, and for Transgender people alone it's 218 per cent. Back in 2020, a survey was carried out in which a third of Queer people who responded reported to have a disability, compared to around twenty-four per cent of the general population. You will find more Disabled people among the LGBTQ+ community than the cisgender heterosexual population, and more Queer people within the Disabled community than in the equivalent group outside of it. This is surprising to some who assume that the numbers would be broadly the same, because these figures aren't represented within the groups they know. There is a paternalistic assumption among a lot of people (not just the Queer community) that Disabled people don't desire sexual and romantic relationships, but also that they would be physically unable to participate in sexual activities, even if they wanted to. Naturally, if someone sees you as incapable of participating in sex, then they may not consider you as a sexual or romantic prospect at all. As a result, many Disabled people report that they feel as though they are not truly a part of the Queer community, seen to be a mascot rather than a member.

A common issue that has cropped up in recent years is

accessibility at Pride events and Queer venues. Historically, many of these venues were 'underground', both figuratively and literally, and so contain stairs and inaccessible structures, and very few changes have been made to accommodate Disabled people. It's unsurprising then that the Queer community has tried so hard to distance itself from disability. As we will cover in later chapters, it wasn't all that long ago that Queerness was considered an illness, and much of the fight for the civil rights of LGBTQ+ people has been focussed on the need to prove that Queer people don't need to be, and can't be, cured. Now of course we would say that Disabled people don't need to be cured either, but the idea of not wanting a cure for an illness is something that many people still struggle with.

There is similar Queerphobia within the Disabled community and particularly among those who Disabled people often interact with, such as carers, parents or personal assistants who control so much of some Disabled people's lives. Having to hide your sexuality or gender identity due to a personal assistant who hates Queer people is often a necessity, when they are the one doing your necessary medical care and keeping you clean and fed. There is an opinion among many people that women are more understanding of disability and impairment than men, and so they assume that they can find companionship. Disabled women are making the deliberate choice to date other women for companionship. Queer people with learning disabilities are often assumed to not have the mental capacity to recognise themselves as being Queer, implying that being LGBTQ+ is something you can decide to be with enough thought and understanding. It probably isn't too surprising that Transgender disabled people have a particularly hard time. Common transphobia rears its head within the Disabled community, but it's often compounded by medical complications that impede or even prevent a person's physical transition with prescribed hormones or surgery. While no one is required to accept these recommendations in order to be 'trans enough', any visible sign of someone's gender non-conformity places them in danger. This danger is emphasised by statistics showing that people who are both Disabled and Queer are significantly more likely to be the victims of a violent crime, as well as a double dose of discrimination. This is before we mention the sheer number of victims of police violence in the US against Disabled people, or those with mental illnesses. By allowing homophobia and transphobia within the Disabled community, and ableism within the Queer community, we exclude people who should be uplifting and safeguarding our communities for the better, and for people who need a caring and compassionate connection.

I note much of this is the same for those from other marginalised groups, such as different racial groups, ethnic groups, nationalities, social classes and religions. This is not from personal or academic experience and so I am not the person to consider that phenomenon.

Queer Disabled people are more likely to endure medical abuse, particularly the denial of necessary medical care, and be bullied at school and discriminated against at work. They are also more likely to live in poverty and be socially isolated. Even as two separate communities, we have a wealth of shared experiences. We're both at high risk of being rejected by our families or caretakers, tend to grow up separated from other people like us, and have, historically, experienced forced medical treatments to suppress our fertility. We have been similarly targeted by those who wish to wipe out undesirables and have had to work hard to create a community of people who understand our needs.

In more recent years, Frida Kahlo may have been separated into her component parts in order to solidify her status as a female, Queer & Disabled icon. The direction of her life was determined by all of each of those things together, as it is for most people who share multiple identities. She was born in 1907, although she would later tell people she'd been born three years later, so they would associate her with the Mexican Revolution that began in 1910. Her father was a European photographer, and her mother was Mexican with Native-American heritage. She helped her father in his photography studio, developing a great eye for detail and composition, She became very close to him, although she did mask his true background later in life. He had moved to Mexico and taken the name 'Guillermo', as the closest alternative to his birth name 'William'. His university career ended after developing epilepsy from a nasty accident. Kahlo's relationship with her mother was far more tense. Sadly, both of her parents were melancholic and frequently sick. As a young child, Frida had taken drawing lessons with a friend of her father's, but didn't see it as a viable career. She started school later than other children her age after developing polio and needing to be isolated from her friends. As a result of the polio infection, her right leg became smaller and thinner, and she was bullied by the other children at school because of it. Her father, however, was able to share this experience of disability with her, helping her navigate it and cope with other people's reactions. He encouraged her to take part in sports and to embrace art, even if she never believed she could make a living out of it. She was a talented scientist, and although she'd had unhappy experiences in other schools, she started at the prestigious *Escuela Nacional Preparatoria* (National Preparatory School) aiming to become a doctor. It was here that she met Diego Rivera for the first time, while he was painting a mural. This school was a fertile breeding ground for the great and the good, and her friendship group consisted of people who would go on to become leading and influential intellectuals of post-revolutionary Mexico. They were anti-conservative and rebellious, but unlike Frida's previous schools, this behaviour was, if not encouraged, accepted as harmless and the acts of young adults discovering who they were. When she was eighteen, Frida and her boyfriend boarded an overcrowded bus home from school. The impatient bus driver attempted to pass a tram coming towards them from the other direction on a very narrow road. The tram crashed into the bus, killing several passengers and seriously injuring Frida. 'The way a sword pierces a bull', an iron handrail from the bus twisted out of shape and impaled her, puncturing her abdomen. It broke her spine, her pelvis, her leg, and collarbone and pierced her uterus, but miraculously missed her other organs. Her boyfriend and fellow passengers removed the handrail from her body at the scene before she was taken to hospital. Fortunately, Frida recovered from her injuries. She spent a month in hospital and two months convalescing at home, which is incredible considering how serious the injury was. The chronic pain remained with her for the rest of her life; one of her friends remarked that she 'lived dying'. She was prescribed further bedrest once the doctors realised the damage to her spine was more extensive than originally diagnosed. She was forced to give up her plan to study medicine and become a doctor. While on three-month's bedrest, her parents encouraged her to paint to pass the time. Her mother rigged an easel up to hang over her bed, and her father gave her paints and affixed a mirror so she could paint self-portraits. In these early days she painted many portraits of her family, but as time passed, she preferred self-portraits, saying, 'I paint myself because I am often alone, and I am the subject I know best.'

Throughout her life, Frida's art served as a poignant reminder of her chronic struggles with emotional and physical pain. She spent most of her life undergoing further treatment and surgeries from doctors who claimed they would be able to restore the health and mobility she had enjoyed as a teenager. Due to her serious injuries she had several miscarriages, and her feelings of guilt were reflected in her paintings. Many of Frida's artworks are characterised by vivid depictions of wounds and blood, which serves as a visual metaphor for her own physical and emotional struggles. Her works often include symbolism from both traditional Mexican, Western and Christian iconographies, reflecting the complexities of her cultural heritage and the merging of her personal and political experiences Her art is renowned for its deeper meanings, with many of her pieces containing subtle metaphors that speak to her nuanced observations of culture and politics during this period. However, many critics dismissed this possibility, implying her work to be naive because of her being a woman. Much of the symbolism regarding her disability revolved around the guilt she felt because her body was unable to perform as she thought it should. She was fearful of being a burden, letting people down and them getting tired of having to care for her. This fear is particularly harmful when it leads individuals to doubt their own worth and potential, and it is common for many Disabled people.

Many of us rethink this mindset when we learn about the social model of disability. This model stands in direct contrast to the medical model of disability, which tells us that our disability is caused by part of our body's inability to function properly, and the only treatment for disability is an advance in medical science. The social model works on the basis that the only reason we are Disabled is because the environment is inaccessible. In contrast, the medical model regards disability as the result of physical impairments, suggesting the only solution to disability is medical advancements. For example, under the medical model we think a wheelchair user is Disabled because they cannot walk up the steps to enter any shops. However, if there was a ramp to get into the building, a wheelchair user would never be prevented from accessing it and wouldn't be unable to go shopping. The fault is not with the individual or the disabled body part, it is with society. This is why many of us who follow the social model, strongly feel that calling someone 'Disabled' is not an insult, but is purely an accurate term and an important descriptor of a part of our identity. It's also why I and many others capitalise the word 'Disabled', and I do so throughout this book. Similarly, the social model highlights the difference between an impairment (for example, a medical diagnosis) and a disability (a way to describe an identity we share because of the way we are treated by others). This is why many Disabled people who ascribe to the social model strongly prefer to be called a Disabled Person rather than a Person with a Disability, but may object to being called a descriptor for their diagnosis (for example, 'a diabetic', 'an amputee' or 'an epileptic'). However, this preference can vary depending on where in the world you are, and I'm very aware that opinions on this topic are diverse and can vary significantly from person to person. The social model was coined in the 1980s in Britain, which may explain why most Disabled organisations and governments use it. However, the concept of the social model is much older. In fact, I've found references from the eighteenth century that describe what we would understand to be the social model. Harriet Martineau demonstrated her understanding of this concept in the mid-nineteenth century. Alf Morris, a politician and disability rights campaigner, discussed this issue for the first time when he tried to bring anti-discriminatory legislation to the British Parliament in 1969. An early disability rights organisation in the United Kingdom, the Union of the Physically Impaired Against Segregation, began discussing the social definition of disability, which was developed by the academic Mike Oliver into the social model of disability in 1983. There has been criticism of the perceived inflexibility of the social model towards certain impairments which feature an amount of physical suffering, for example chronic pain conditions. However, many proponents of the social model believe that it allows for that flexibility, as at no point does the social model mean that someone isn't experiencing unpleasant symptoms, just that they are not the reason someone is unable to participate in society. For example, if employers, education facilities, businesses, medical professionals and individuals were more flexible with everyone, then people with chronic pain could delay handing in homework until they're out of a flare up, work from home when needed to avoid commuting in pain, or have shops deliver if they can't go out. Neither of these options would reduce pain levels, but they would enable people with chronic pain to participate in society more easily, without being forced to perform as non-disabled people do. This highlights the stark reality that Disabled, chronically ill, and neurodiverse communities have been underserved by society. Frida Kahlo's experience is a poignant reminder of this. Once she had sufficiently recovered from the injuries she sustained in the bus crash, she began hanging out with her friends from school. Most of her friends were studying at university now, which made Frida feel like she'd been left behind by her peers, but she was fascinated by the political activists they knew, and soon joined the Mexican Communist Party to campaign alongside them. At one of these gatherings of the most fashionable communists in Mexico, Frida once again met Diego Rivera. She asked him to look over some of her artwork and see if she was good enough to be an artist. While she was recovering, she had briefly considered becoming a medical illustrator, but she preferred the creative freedom of deciding what to paint for herself. Diego was impressed, saying, 'it was obvious to me that this girl was an authentic artist'. They soon began dating – which her parents weren't all that thrilled about considering he was twenty-one years her senior – and married a year later. Her parents objected to the marriage, since Diego was already involved in at least two other relationships, but they did concede he had plenty of money with which to support Frida, who needed help paying for all the medical treatment she needed. Soon they moved out of Mexico – as many people from different career backgrounds did – to start anew in San Francisco. They were already well known both at home and abroad by then, being referred to as simply 'Diego and Frida' by the Mexican media. Mexico, however, would always remain a significant part of Frida's identity. She was supposedly born in the same house where she later died and returned to Mexico whenever she could. She began wearing traditional indigenous Mexican outfits after she married, as did several other progressive women in the country at the time. The post-revolutionary mood was one of pride in their national identity and an appreciation of traditional culture which was encouraged by Frida's school. The school strongly promoted a political ideology which emphasised pride for all things Mexican and a rejection of colonial ideals. She started adopting traditional folk-art techniques within her paintings, and many people credit her with the rest of the world's awareness of traditional Mexican folk art. Her artwork is considered so important to the cultural heritage and identity that her paintings have been prohibited from being moved out of the country. That's not to say that she hated living anywhere outside of Mexico. She was popular in the States due to her excellent English and style, but she quickly became tired of being seen as Diego's wife, telling a reporter that 'of course he [Rivera] does well for a little boy, but it is I who am the big artist'. She enjoyed America, although she didn't like the levels of inequality and having to hang out with capitalists. When discussing history, particularly niche topics like Disability and Queer history, it's common to concentrate on the Western hemisphere. In Disability history, this focus is often reduced even further to the United Kingdom and the US. It can be significantly harder to find sources that discuss Disabled figures, especially those where Disabled people are speaking for themselves. As a British English speaker, I am more aware of the history in my own country, and restricted to sources written in English or translated. I've made an effort to cover a diverse range of people in this book, but I've inevitably fallen short when it comes to global representation.

Diego was taken on mural projects across America, accompanied by Frida. During their downtime, they engaged in numerous extramarital affairs. While Diego had relationships with women, including with Frida's sister on one occasion, Frida had affairs with both men and women. According to accounts, Diego was unperturbed by Frida's relationships with women but became jealous when she had affairs with men. Her most famous affair was with Leon Trotsky. Some sources claim that several women Diego had relationships with, also ended up in Frida's bed. Besides her bisexuality and newfound status as a Queer icon, Frida also had a fluid sense of gender identity. She frequently painted herself as a man in her art and even wore male clothing as a child. Frida's art often featured nude women in intimate settings, and she never hid her relationships with women within her social circle.

After their return from America, her health had continued to deteriorate. The tension from their numerous affairs and Diego's resentment and jealousy ultimately led to their divorce. However, they remarried soon after. Despite undergoing multiple unsuccessful surgeries on her spine, Frida remained determined to support herself through her art. Unfortunately, her poor health forced her to attend one of her exhibitions from a mobile bed, and she soon became largely confined to her home. Frida's health continued to decline, and she eventually underwent leg amputation surgery due to gangrene. However, she still struggled with numerous infections that threatened to overwhelm her body. Frida's death on 13 July 1954 was shrouded in mystery. Although the official cause was listed as a pulmonary embolism, many people believed she had taken an overdose of painkillers, knowing her end was near. In her final note, Frida wrote: 'I joyfully await the exit – and I hope never to return – Frida.'

The home where Frida grew up and spent her final years was converted into a museum dedicated to her art and her work. The museum opened in 1958, a year after Diego's death. He had described Frida's passing as 'the most tragic day of my life'. Frida's life was marked by her extraordinary popularity, even during her lifetime. When she passed away, she was honoured with a state funeral under the communist flag. Despite her fame during her lifetime, Frida was primarily known as 'Diego's wife', until the 1970s when several books about her life were published. This led to a newfound interest in her life and art among art historians and feminist academics. Frida's unique style and life story made it easy for her to become an enduring cultural phenomenon. Her striking appearance and compelling life story resonated with people, who felt an emotional connection with her. This empathy may have been difficult for her to fathom, given her years of isolation due to her health issues and personal struggles. As Frida herself said, she was 'the main character of her own mythology, as a woman, as a Mexican, and as a suffering person'.

By examining Frida's life, we can see how these two histories intersect and how they inform each other. This collision helps us to understand the complexities of power, identity, and experience. Considering these histories together can reveal a deeper understanding of the ways in which marginalised communities have been impacted by societal attitudes and policies.

Marsha P. Johnson

'The fairies were not supposed to riot'

Marsha P. Johnson is now widely recognised as a pioneer of the Queer movement, and her story has been shared extensively online. However, it's worth questioning whether all these stories are entirely accurate. Marsha's journey of self-discovery began after she moved to New York and became part of the vibrant Queer community. During this time, she experimented with different identities, eventually settling on being seen as a gay man, transvestite, or a drag queen. By exploring the complexities of Marsha's identity, we can gain a deeper understanding of the fluidity of gender and sexuality, and the ways in which people have navigated their own identities throughout history. Many people are familiar with Marsha P. Johnson as a prominent transgender figure, but new information may challenge our understanding of her identity. It's important to consider that while the term 'transgender' wasn't widely used during her time, she and her community did have specific language and definitions to describe gender flexibility. These terminologies can provide insight into how Marsha might have understood herself, and her views of gender. By examining the language and definitions used during her time, we gain a deeper understanding of her identity and the ways in which she navigated gender. Marsha P. Johnson was instrumental in distinguishing between transsexual and transvestite identities. She defined transsexuals as individuals who were assigned a gender at birth that didn't match their true identity, and who may seek medical treatment to align their gender with their identity. In contrast, she described transvestites as individuals who were often masculine-looking, but still identified as male. Interestingly, Marsha herself still used a female name in her daily life despite her masculine appearance. Her friend Sylvia Rivera held a different view on the term, believing that it could be used by gay men who enjoyed dressing in women's clothes. According to Sylvia, straight people who cross-dressed were not transvestites, but simply cross-dressers. The distinction between transsexual and transvestite identities has led some people to speculate that Marsha might have identified more closely with the terms gender fluid or gender non-conforming. Marsha used she/her pronouns when referring to herself, but occasionally returned to her birth name Malcolm for short periods. Although it's possible that Johnson's pronouns might have been they/them if they were widely used at the time, my only reference point is Marsha's own use of she/her pronouns. I will use she/her throughout, including when referring to Marsha or Malcolm.

Marsha was born in New Jersey, to a religious family. When she was just 5 years old, she discovered her love of dressing up in women's clothes, which deeply upset and disturbed her family. For Marsha, being gay didn't seem like a realistic option in real life. In her household, openly loving another man was considered unthinkable, like a fantasy. However, Marsha believed that her family's disapproval stemmed from ignorance rather than hatred. But Marsha's mother soon shifted her view, urging Marsha to find a wealthy partner to support her. Raised in the Episcopal Church alongside her siblings, Marsha developed a strong affinity for her faith. She claimed to have 'married' Jesus Christ at the age of 16 while still in high school, an experience that seemed to deepen her devotion. As she left home, Marsha retained her faith, saying she had taken God with her wherever she went. However, she didn't limit herself to her childhood church; she also attended Catholic churches, Greek Orthodox ceremonies, and Jewish synagogues because, she said, she was, 'covering all angles'.

A sexual assault made her discard the clothes she felt most comfortable in, and she decided to keep her true identity hidden until she could escape the town. At 17, she left home for New York with just $15 and a bag of clothes, got a job as a waitress and made the transition to wearing female clothing permanent. After trying out different names, Marsha finally settled on her new identity. When she chose the name Marsha P. Johnson, she decided that the middle initial would stand for the phrase 'pay it no mind', allowing her to tell others who asked too many questions about her gender or clothing to mind their own business. Marsha had a joke that she loved telling, and she once even managed to get out of jail using her middle initial as a punchline. A judge found it amusing enough to order her release. She moved to Greenwich Village, the heart of the gay community, where she publicly declared her sexuality and transformed her life. After that, she said her whole life was built around sex and gay liberation, as well as being a drag queen. In an interview, she recalled that before becoming a drag queen, she felt like nobody from nowhere. Most of her drag performances were political, satirical, and comedic - not surprising given her distaste for the highbrow culture and pretentiousness. She loved creating outfits using men's clothes, women's clothes, and items she found on the streets. She enjoyed confusing people. Marsha delighted in shocking people by adopting different personas.

However, she didn't consistently retain the persona; instead, she would occasionally present herself as Malcom. On those occasions, many people noticed that her more aggressive and violent side would emerge. Malcom was actually banned from several gay bars around Christopher Street. It's natural to assume that Malcom was banned because Marsha was not presenting herself as her true self, which led to feelings of anger. Some friends believed this was the case. However, others thought that Malcom's behaviour was a result of Marsha's mental illness, which caused her to dress differently. Some of Marsha's friends have described her as having a 'schizophrenic personality', but it's unclear whether she had any official diagnosis. Marsha was detained by the police or hospitalised several times, often requiring her friends to intervene and persuade hospital staff to release her into their care. According to Marsha, she experienced eight episodes of breakdown by 1979. During these episodes, she could become violent and was banned from various places for fighting with others. She explained that she didn't enjoy getting into fights, but when she was forced to leave a place without knowing why, she became violent. During her breakdowns, she often encountered strangers who didn't understand the LGBTQ+ community. Marsha's life was precarious, as was that of many others in the Queer community during this time. For much of her time in New York, she did not have a stable home, often sleeping on benches or staying in hotels and living with friends. Her sex work put her in dangerous situations, and despite the city's diversity, New York City was not a safe place for LGBTQ+ individuals. The police frequently targeted individuals who appeared to be LGBTQ+, attempting to arrest or even harm them. In the 1960s, the New York State Liquor Authority refused to grant licences to gay bars. The Mafia saw an opportunity to make money by taking over the gay bars in Greenwich Village. By the mid-60s, they had acquired most of the gay bars, paying bribes to the police to avoid raids. In 1966, they purchased the Stonewall Inn, a previously unsuccessful restaurant and transformed it into the one gay bar in town that allowed dancing. The Mafia ran Stonewall as a 'members only bottle shop' to avoid needing a liquor licence. This meant that patrons had to be members to gain entry, but this was just a formality. If you looked gay enough or were recognised by the bouncer, you were allowed in and simply had to sign your name in a book. Unsurprisingly people didn't use their real names. In the years since, many have suggested that the Mafia's real profit came from blackmailing wealthy clients, rather than from the volume of business or exorbitant prices for watered down drinks. Despite the police bribes, raids were frequent and had become routine. Raids involved flashing white lights, checking identity cards, and arresting the bar staff, people in drag or women wearing fewer than three items of 'female clothing'. Most drinks were stored off-site, allowing the bar to reopen quickly if needed. However, 28 June 1969, things didn't go according to plan.

Many have credited Marsha with throwing the first brick at the Stonewall Riots, but she denied being there at the beginning. It's possible she denied being there due to her previous encounters with the police. However, it seems more likely that she was telling the truth and simply wasn't there. She was a significant figure in both the uprisings and the bar's history as one of the first drag queens to frequent the Stonewall Inn after they stopped barring gay men. The riots on Christopher Street that night were the culmination of fast-growing tension between the LGBTQ+ community and the police. After the number of violent raids on these gay bars had increased exponentially, the community had decided that enough was enough. The bar that night was bustling with people growing restless as time passed. They had grown accustomed to receiving a tip-off about impending raids, but this time there was none. Patrons were frustrated and annoyed as they lined up in front of police, ready to produce their identification. However, many of them refused to hand it over. With the anger mounting, those who were released refused to go home. Instead, they stayed outside the bar, growing more and more incensed on behalf of their friends still inside. The police, realising their efforts were only fuelling the flames, decided to take drastic action. They arrested everyone who refused to cooperate, but by this point, word of the raid and the defiance had already spread beyond the Stonewall Inn's walls. When the police emerged from the bar to take the arrested customers away, they were shocked to find that the crowd had swelled to ten times its original size. When Stormé DeLarverie was struck with a baton for complaining about her handcuffs being too tight, a collective feeling of displeasure spread among the crowd. The phrase 'we've had enough of this crap' was on everyone's lips. Reportedly, the police began beating both the arrested individuals and the onlookers. This action sparked the riots. The New York Police Department's tactical response team turned up to free the police officers who had by this point barricaded themselves inside the Stonewall Inn. One eyewitness said that the police attitude quickly turned from concern to anger. 'They were humiliated … Everybody else had rioted ... but the fairies were not supposed to riot'. The police were furious about the aggressive resistance, especially that part of the group the called 'transvestites' who they described as 'fighting furiously'. The rioters proceeded to spend the entire night pushing against the police in such a hilariously camp way that it only further infuriated them. The rioters formed a giant kick line to prevent the police from clearing the streets, singing songs from musicals as they ran away from the police, only to run around the block and appear behind them. While Marsha denies being there right at the start, she was there later, saying in interviews afterwards that she heard about the riots and decided to join. She decided to go down to the building, despite arriving at 2 am, when the flames had already engulfed the structure. The first night of rioting finally came to an end around 4 am. The next day some people paid their respects, while others stopped out of curiosity to look at the destroyed Stonewall Inn. As the day wore on, the mood of resistance didn't waver. By nightfall, thousands of people had gathered, screening cars to check if drivers supported the cause. The streets were filled with people from all walks of life, united in their defiance. Marsha P. Johnson took matters into her own hands on the second night. She climbed up a lamppost and dropped her handbag, which contained a brick, onto a police car. The flames from nearby rubbish bin fires illuminated the scene, creating an unforgettable image. The police struggled to contain the riots on their own, and they continued sporadically for several days until the rioters began exploring alternatives to advance their cause. It soon became clear that the gay community in New York was not going to back down, and they were determined to organise and end the discrimination. The Stonewall Inn itself, however, did not survive the aftermath. By October, it was up for rent. Today, however, the building has been purchased and restored as a historic landmark and a popular gay bar.

The year after the Stonewall Riots, parades had spread to the UK, Sweden, and France. The riots had sparked a change in approach, as people moved away from tactics like setting fire to bins or trying to present themselves as non-combative. One year later, in commemoration of the riots, the Christopher Street Liberation Day in New York marked the anniversary, with other marches in Chicago and Los Angeles. This shift was reflected in the founding of the Gay Liberation Front. Marsha P. Johnson and her long-time friend Sylvia Rivera joined the Drag Queen section of the Gay Liberation Front. In 1970, they played a key role in forming STAR, the Street Transvestite Action Revolutionaries, following a protest against the

University of New York's decision to cancel an event allegedly due to its sponsorship by gay organisations. The 'Street Transvestites' were the last protesters standing at the Stonewall Riots. The experience convinced them that they needed to focus on their own community and the gay rights movement as a whole. STAR was formed to provide housing for homeless gay people, including those who identified as 'street queens.' They also supported gay prisoners and others in difficult living situations who wrote letters to connect with others who felt like them. After fundraising, STAR was able to secure a four-bedroom flat in a rundown part of town. The organisation used this space to house vulnerable people they met on the streets. Marsha and Sylvia took to the streets, engaging in sex work to support themselves and ensure that their younger friends didn't have to resort to the same means. Despite their initial efforts, STAR house didn't thrive as a financially sustainable venture. The organisation's work continued, inspiring others to set up similar projects, but ultimately, their focus shifted. However, their campaigning didn't go unnoticed. At the 1973 Christopher Street Liberation Day Parade, STAR and other groups were asked to march at the back of the parade because they were perceived as giving the Gay Pride movement a bad name by trying to present themselves as normal and reasonable. The group was outraged by this decision and decided to take matters into their own hands. Instead of marching at the back, they marched at the front of the parade, with Sylvia later storming the stage to deliver a powerful speech about the importance of inclusivity and solidarity within the LGBTQ+ community. After that, Marsha and Sylvia both drifted away from the mainstream gay rights movement. They felt rejected and discarded by a community they had given so much to. Marsha eventually moved in with a friend, who initially invited her to stay for one night but ended up becoming her long-term residence. She lived there for 12 years, the longest period of residence aside from her parent's home. It was during this time that Marsha discovered she was HIV positive, and many of her friends were also being diagnosed with the same virus. During the early days of the AIDS crisis, a lack of information, fear and ignorance led to widespread stigma and discrimination. Marsha cared for many of her friends, both at their homes and in hospitals as they began to fall ill. Despite the risks and challenges she faced, she remained devoted to those around her, providing emotional support and practical care during a time of great need. As Marsha became more involved in the HIV/AIDS movement, she began to work with various activist groups to raise awareness about the virus and its symptoms. She also focused on ensuring that those affected by the disease received both medical and emotional care. The disease was terrifying for many patients, who had no known cause and watched as their loved ones succumbed to its devastating effects. Marsha's most prominent affiliation was with ACT UP, an organisation dedicated to unleashing power against AIDS. ACT UP's primary focus was on medical research, striving to find effective treatments and campaigning for patient access to these treatments. Additionally, they worked to influence government policies and legislation to better support those affected by HIV/AIDS. ACT UP was different from other organisations like the Gay Men's Health Crisis because while they were mostly focussed on a community response to individual patients with support and care, ACT UP was targeting pharmaceutical companies, hospitals and politicians who were either not taking HIV/AIDS seriously, or actively harming patients. While GHMC's work was certainly significant, it's worth noting that their contributions were not diminished by ACT UP's efforts. In fact, GHMC is credited with establishing the world's first AIDS hotline, which was initially run from a volunteer's home. The hotline received an overwhelming 100 messages on its first day, and for a long time, it served as the primary means of disseminating information about HIV/AIDS. The hotline provided vital information on how to treat the disease, prevent transmission, and exercise patient rights. Eventually, the volume of calls became too much for the volunteer's home line, and GMHC established its own organisational phone line to handle the demand. During this event, ACT UP members marched in Washington to demand equal rights and recognition for gay and lesbian individuals. While ACT UP was active in Washington, chapters of the organisation were also established around the world. The New York chapter Marsha was part of was particularly notable for its memorable protests. In 1989, members chained themselves to the New York Stock Exchange to protest the high cost of the one approved treatment for AIDS. The action was a bold statement against the pharmaceutical companies that profited from the disease. The following year, ACT UP members shut down the FDA building for a full day, demanding that more patients be allowed to access experimental AIDS drugs on a compassionate basis. Just before Christmas in 1989, 111 protestors were arrested in St Patrick's Cathedral after staging a 'die-in' to protest the Catholic Church's opposition to safe sex education, and its public condemnation of homosexuality. The dramatic scene, which saw protesters collapse to the floor in protest, shocked bystanders and drew attention to the cause. ACT UP's activism wasn't limited to high profile protests. They were also working on more subtle, yet impactful initiatives. One notable example was their challenge to *Cosmo* magazine's publication of an article claiming that healthy genitals made it possible for women to contract AIDS from their HIV positive partners. The article was riddled with misinformation and errors, and ACT UP's pressure ultimately led to its retraction. *Cosmo* initially resisted taking action, citing the fact that a doctor had written the article. However, after being challenged on the harm they were causing women by allowing the article to stand, they eventually relented. Following their success in getting *Cosmo* to retract the article, ACT UP turned their attention to the Centre for Disease Control's official definitions of AIDS. The CDC's definitions were so specific that they essentially excluded women from being diagnosed with AIDS. As a result of this distinction, women were not eligible for social security benefits and other resources related to AIDS. You may not know that ACT UP's most well-known action was their own activism. They were passed the responsibility of the SILENCE=DEATH project, a striking and provocative visual poster that deliberately linked the refusal of the establishment to acknowledge AIDS to the devastating number of lives lost. The poster was starkly black, with an upside-down pink triangle emblazoned above the text. The pink triangle was deliberately chosen for its association with the Nazi regime's persecution and execution of gay people, serving as a powerful reminder of the parallels between historical oppression and modern-day struggles. The activism of the time undoubtedly made a significant difference, given the limited treatment options and the devastating impact on those affected by AIDS. However, there was a notable shortage of AIDS activism by people with AIDS themselves. Aside from a few individual activists who shared their experiences with the media, there were few patient advocacy groups. This led to many people with AIDS feeling like they were experiencing a 'social death' as they were often treated as if they were lost causes, already dead.

In the early days of the disease, many people who later tested positive for AIDS were initially diagnosed with rare forms of cancer caused by AIDS. As a result, patient groups were established by cancer organisations, which may have contributed to the widespread perception of AIDS as 'gay cancer'. While this name may have been misinformed and stigmatising, it wasn't necessarily driven towards the disease or its patients. Many early groups formed in response to AIDS were primarily support groups, where patients began researching and exploring theories about the causes of the disease. For people with chronic illnesses, this process is often a way to cope with their new circumstances. However, much of the early activism by people with AIDS was focused on making themselves visible. They sought to remind the rest of the gay community that they were still alive, still present, and still deserving of respect and dignity. Many people with AIDS felt that their community was either ignoring them or treating them as a sob story, perpetuating harmful stereotypes. They were often dismissed by others who believed they didn't have a right to contribute to the conversation about AIDS simply because they were sick. One person was told that their sole contribution to the gay community was their illness.

This message was echoed by others who believed that people with AIDS had no value or contribution to offer beyond the illness. Despite these challenges, people with AIDS organised themselves and took action. The most notable example was the 1983 candlelight march, which took place simultaneously in San Francisco and New York. The march aimed to 'humanise the AIDS crisis and make people with AIDS more visible. The event's success was marked by its enduring impact, with images of the march surviving to this day. In San Francisco, the march took the same route as the memorial march for Harvey Milk, a few years earlier. The similarity was not lost on many people, who saw parallels between the struggles of those who were remembered with honour. In 1983, a group of gay men with AIDS from across the country came together at a conference to draft a document that would guide doctors, patients, and the public on how to treat people with AIDS. The resulting document, known as the Denver Principles, reflected a profound understanding of the social model of disability. The Denver Principles emphasised the importance of self-representation, inclusion in decision-making, and autonomy over treatment choices. Perhaps most importantly, they sought to affirm the dignity of people with AIDS, rejecting labels like 'victim' or 'patient' in favour of their own identity as people with AIDS. In contrast to the prevailing attitude in gay literature at the time, many people with AIDS felt that they were being erased from their identity as gay men. Instead of being seen as individuals living with AIDS, they were reduced to being mere 'AIDS victims'. This erasure was perpetuated by the lack of attention from governmental officials, including President Ronald Regan, who didn't publicly address AIDS until 1985. Despite these challenges, activists continued to campaign for anti-discrimination legislation and improved medical care. However, it became clear that the only way to achieve these goals was to work in tandem with disability rights advocates fighting for similar civil rights laws. For many people with AIDS, this realisation was difficult to accept. They had spent years trying to distance themselves from the label of disability, and now they were forced to confront the reality that their struggles were not unique to their community. In recent years, a piece of AIDS activism has resonated deeply with the public, despite not originating as traditional activism. The idea was sparked by the candlelight march in 1985, where posters listed the names of 1,000 men who had died of AIDS. Friends, families, and colleagues were invited to create fabric panels that would be sewn together into a quilt, each measuring three feet by six feet, the size of an average grave. For many people, this quilt panel served as a substitute for a traditional funeral or memorial service; due to familial shame and funeral homes' reluctance to handle the bodies of people with AIDS, many had no traditional funeral service. This powerful project provided a sense of community and recognition for those affected by AIDS, and its impact continues to be felt today. Marsha was actively involved in creating quilt panels for friends who had lost loved ones to AIDS. She also attended numerous demonstrations and memorial services, including those organised by ACT UP and Gay Men's Health Crisis, as well as interfaith memorial services. Throughout her time advocating for the rights of people with AIDS, Marsha dedicated herself to ensuring that those affected by the disease would not be forgotten.

In 1992, Marsha's body was found floating in the Hudson River. The police conducted a cursory investigation, ruled her death a suicide and closed the case without much scrutiny. Her closest friends were sceptical of the official outcome, and subsequent investigations revealed significant evidence of foul play. The Netflix documentary 'The Death and Life of Marsha P. Johnson' detailed the findings of these investigations, which included an initial report suggesting homicide as a possible cause of death. The police were reluctant to pursue any leads or interview witnesses, and many people with knowledge of Marsha's life were never spoken to. Instead, it was left to friends and non-profit organisations to piece together the circumstances surrounding Marsha's death. The frequency of queer bashing crimes in New York City during this time made it unsurprising that the police failed to prioritise an investigation into Marsha's death. Before her death, Marsha participated in protests to address the very issue that led to her own death. Marsha's body was cremated following a small church ceremony, and her community marched back to the Hudson River to scatter her ashes. The police eventually closed the street where the procession took place, realising they couldn't stop the crowd from blocking the road. However, their visible presence at her memorial, following their failure to investigate Marsha's death, only added to the community's outrage and anger.

No matter what she did for the Queer community, the homeless population, those with HIV and AIDS and the victims of homophobic crime, the police viewed her as a mentally ill street queen, and assumed no one would notice she was gone. Her impact on the community's response to the AIDS pandemic, and her commitment to trans people's inclusion within the Queer liberation movement, meant that she is remembered as a vital figure in both Disability and Queer history.

Kitty Cone

'Their goals were unfeasible and their lifestyles improper'

In 2020 Netflix released a new type of documentary which set the world ablaze. At first it was the Disabled community, but it eventually spread to able bodied people too. The documentary covered and exposed a community which many people never considered had a story of their own. *Crip Camp: A Disabled Revolution* covered a history that many people were totally unaware of. The passing by the Americans of Disabilities Act, an anti-discrimination law to protect Disabled people, was seen by many people as either an inevitability of the tide of civil rights legislation or a kindness gifted to the impaired.

It never occurred to people that the Disabled community had had to fight so hard. The documentary went on to be nominated for an Oscar, won numerous other awards, and educated hundreds of thousands of people on a small part of disability history. Disability activists became household names, and many individuals became aware of Disabled people as a distinct group, with their own identity, community and history. This is a universal experience for many, disabled during their childhood and adolescence, and one that the campers featured in Crip Camp couldn't avoid.

Kitty Cone was one of many Disabled people who experienced discrimination from childhood. Born on 7 April 1944 into a wealthy military family, she had a nomadic childhood, attending multiple schools. As a young child, she was misdiagnosed with Cerebral Palsy, and it wasn't until she was 15 years old that the correct diagnosis was made. In fact, she was living with muscular dystrophy, a condition that was vastly different from the initial diagnosis. At that point, her prognosis was dire, it was predicted she wouldn't survive beyond 20 years old. Despite these bleak predictions, Kitty remained optimistic and continued to live life to the fullest. Her determination was fuelled by the recognition that her health was not defined by her condition. Kitty first became aware of the discrimination during her early years at a private girls boarding school run by the church. It would follow her throughout her life. As a student, she used a walking stick to navigate the old, traditional buildings on campus. However, this accommodation was not enough to spare her from the unfair treatment she received at the hands of the headmistress, who imposed rules on her that were not required of her peers. She was instructed to bathe separately from the three other girls in her dorm, citing the need for a private tub. However, the large outdoor tub proved inaccessible to her, as she was unable to exit it on her own. In response, she decided that this restriction was unreasonable and began to use the same bath as her peers. This defiance of rules became a hallmark of her behaviour during her time at that school, where she continued to disregard activities that had been previously denied her. In a predictable yet poignant outcome, the headmistress ultimately expelled Kitty, given the concerted effort to exclude her from the school community. In retrospect, Kitty speculated that the reason was likely due to the headmistress's concern about liability, as she had imposed numerous prohibitions on her. However, Kitty recognised that these explanations ultimately boiled down to a simple and undeniable fact: that she was Disabled, and the headmistress disapproved of that. This experience sparked her passion for fighting for the rights of Disabled people. Like many activists, Kitty attributed her advocacy to the formative events of her life, stating that her experiences had determined her path as an activist. She believed that her choices had been severely limited by the fact that she had a disability, a sentiment shared by many others who had faced similar challenges. As she looked to the future, she was about to discover how rapidly and profoundly change could occur when like-minded individuals came together. A group of young people attending a summer camp in upstate New York gained a unique advantage. Camp Jened, established in 1951, was a summer camp specifically designed for American teenagers with disabilities, located in the rural countryside of New York state. Initially, the camp operated like a traditional summer camp, employing college students, and former campers, as counsellors, and offering activities for Disabled teenagers. However, it didn't remain ordinary for long. As the camp evolved, it became heavily influenced by the counterculture movement of the 1960s, transforming into a more unstructured and unconventional camp experience. When a social worker with experience in camps for Disabled young people took over, the camp underwent a significant transformation. The recruited counsellors, who had previously been staff members, began to adopt a more collaborative approach, blurring the lines between the campers and staff. The absence of a hierarchical structure allowed for a unique dynamic, where campers enjoyed greater autonomy and freedom. This shift had a profound impact on the non-disabled staff, as they came to understand that the real challenges faced by Disabled were not physical or related to their impairments, but rather stemmed from a society that refused to accommodate their needs.

This relaxed atmosphere at the camp fostered a playful and carefree environment, where pranks and jokes were a natural part of the social dynamics. The documentary features a revealing scene early on, showcasing the Camp Director shirtless, digging holes, as he candidly explains, 'I thought it'd be funny if they tripped', because 'our kids are pretty clumsy.' As the camera pans across the camp, it's clear that the absence of adult supervision has created a unique environment. With teenagers gathering without the usual constraints, romantic relationships blossomed. For many of these young individuals, this was their first opportunity to spend time with others, who shared similar experiences. Free from the constraints of societal expectations and stereotypes, they were able to break free from the stigma and infantilisation that often accompanies the label of 'disabled'. They felt as if the outside world didn't exist. The campers formed romantic relationships, experimented with substances, and developed crucial bonds and networks that would have a profound impact on their lives. For many, the absence of rules was a significant draw. James Lebrecht, the filmmaker, was told by friends that 'you'll probably end up doing dope with the counsellors,' and he thought it sounded like an enticing prospect. In a memorable scene from the film, captured on footage from the 1960s, the campers and counsellors unite to tackle a crisis when someone discovers what they believe to be crab lice in their bunkhouse. With an open environment conducive to political and social discussions, the campers were able to envision a world without barriers and realise that they could challenge the exclusionary society that had long excluded them. Kitty's first venture away from home was to the University of Illinois, where she pursued a degree in English Literature. Notably, she returned to her birthplace, the town of Champaign, to continue her education. Concurrently, she began the activism that would define the trajectory of her life and was subsequently elected to the student senate. She became deeply enthralled with political activism and student advocacy, actively engaging in campaigns to combat racial segregation in local housing. Alongside her peers, she took a stand against this social injustice. Additionally, she joined and became a prominent member of the advocacy group Students for a Democratic Society. However, her life took a devastating turn in 1963 when her mother passed away from throat cancer. In response, Kitty took a semester off from college to return home and grapple with the loss of her mother. Following her semester-long hiatus, Kitty returned to university, but failed to graduate. After leaving college, she remained in Illinois, where she settled in Chicago. There, she worked as an anti-war organiser for the Young Socialist Alliance, an affiliation of the Socialist Workers Party. This involvement, however, led to a rift with her father, who had been a lieutenant in the army, as she became increasingly estranged from him. This development was particularly poignant for Kitty, given her recent loss of her mother, making it a challenging experience for her to come to terms with.

As a young adult, Kitty enjoyed travelling with friends, but her experiences were increasingly marred by the profound lack of accessibility. By this time, she had become reliant on a wheelchair, and the constant obstacles she faced were a significant source of frustration. Whether travelling in South America, Eastern Europe, or back in the United States, she encountered numerous barriers, including narrow doors, buildings without ramps, and buses without lifts. Moreover, many experiences with transportation were particularly challenging, with many instances where her wheelchair was damaged or broken on aeroplanes, resulting in bruising and discomfort. Kitty had struggles with excessive drinking, and by the time she reached her mid-twenties, she had come to realise that she was an alcoholic. She often remarked that her mother, who had also struggled with addiction, was a kindred spirit, and this perceived genetic predisposition led her to acknowledge the problem at an early age. Her childhood experiences, marked by her mother's struggles with alcoholism, had instilled in her a keen awareness of the destructive nature of addiction. It was not until 1979, however, that she began attending Alcoholics

Anonymous meetings, which would become a vital source of support and comfort throughout her life. After enduring many harsh winters in Chicago, Kitty made the decision in 1972 to relocate to California, where she could be closer to her friends and family. While the prospect of warmer weather and not having to shovel snow every day was certainly appealing, it was the opportunity to build a more fulfilling life that ultimately drove her westward. She began working with the Center for Independent Living in Berkeley, leveraging her skills as a campaigner to identify and secure resources and funding that would empower individuals with disabilities to achieve greater independence. The roots of the Center for Independent Living can be traced back to the innovative Cowell Residence Program at the University of California, Berkeley, which pioneered the concept of accommodating students with significant disabilities and care needs. Initially, it was a challenging endeavour to convince the university authorities to implement this programme, as it was perceived as a high-risk venture. However, the initiative proved to be a resounding success, with its impact being immeasurable. In 1962, Ed Roberts, a newly enrolled student, was eager to start his academic journey away from home, engage in learning and connect with fellow new students. Although he had additional complexity to his living arrangements, Ed Roberts' post-polio quadriplegia required him to be constantly enclosed within an iron lung. He became one of the first severely Disabled individuals to be accepted by the University, and his determination to breathe freely while studying led to a unique solution. Due to his insistence that he be able to continue breathing while studying, the university administrators decided that the only practical location for his iron lung (and all his accompanying equipment) would be in the Student Hospital on campus. In 1966 the feasibility of the programme became evident, two additional quadriplegics had joined the Cowell Residence Programme, and within three years, a total of twelve severely Disabled students were living in the programme. Recognising its success, the university officially established the scheme as a recognised university programme and received support from the California Department of Rehabilitation. However, the Disabled students' segregation in the hospital and the inaccessibility of the surrounding town forced them to be largely confined to the campus, where they interacted primarily with one another. Unfortunately for the University, they failed to anticipate the consequences that would unfold next. Many individuals, including politicians, doctors, and leaders, have discovered that when a group of Disabled individuals gather, they share their experiences, express anger, and organise. The students bonded over their shared struggles, with discrimination, inaccessibility, exclusion, and reliance on others. However, their future as advocates was sealed when a new rehabilitation counsellor assigned to the programme attempted to persuade the university to evict two students from their residence, and by extension exclude them from their studies. The justification for this proposal was based solely on her own assumptions and biases, as she deemed the students' educational goals unattainable and their lifestyles unacceptable. Despite the counsellor's initial support from the majority of the programme's staff, the students joined together to resist her efforts, and ultimately defeated her attempt to have the students evicted. The cumulative impact of these incidents, combined with the inevitable passage of time leading up to their graduation, prompted the students to consider how they could continue to advocate for Disabled students after they were no longer actively studying. Many of them began working with the university to establish a more permanent programme for Disabled students. The programme they developed was centred around independent living principles, which prioritised student autonomy and choice. As the programme expanded, the scope of assistance it offered to Disabled individuals at the university grew, and over time, more and more non-students began reaching out for help and guidance. After collectively exploring ways trying to expand their services to the community, the students established the Center for Independent Living in 1972. The centre provided a range of services, including wheelchair repair, assistance finding accessible and affordable housing, and vocational training. However, it quickly developed into a powerful political force, driving many changes in Disability rights in the US since the 1970s. The spark ignited by the Center for Independent Living in Berkeley has coursed through the veins of major developments, from landmark legislation that outlawed discrimination to the nationwide protests against the removal of hard-won rights by court decisions. The Center for Independent Living in Berkeley served as a vibrant hub of knowledge, organisation, and protest, attracting some of the most prominent and influential figures in the Disability rights movement. Judith Heumann, a prominent figure in the Disability rights movement, described Kitty as a 'fireball', noting that her words were like lightning, striking a chord with those who listened and inspiring them to follow her. With years of experience as a campaigner and organiser before many of her peers had even considered entering politics, Kitty brought a unique set of skills to the table, which proved invaluable when the group began to mastermind the 504 Sit-In.

As the Center for Independent Living in Berkeley gained political significance, its staff and many of the figures familiar to those who study Disability history, were largely comprised of former campers from Jened. Given the fertile environment provided by the camp, many of these individuals went on to become politically active at Berkeley, and were deeply involved in the fight to implement Section 504 of the Rehabilitation Act. Eventually, a suitable version of the Americans with Disabilities Act was signed into law.

In the 1970s, American lawmakers decided the need to reform the existing Vocational Rehabilitation Act, shifting its focus towards providing comprehensive assistance for individuals with severe disabilities. As they debated the name for this new legislation, they settled on the Rehabilitation Act 1973, a name that, despite its straightforward title, marked a ground-breaking moment in Disability rights. This new legislation was the first to recognise disabled individuals as a unified group, and it extended civil rights to them for the first time. However, the most innovative and significant aspect of this act for Disabled individuals was section 504. This section specifically stated that, 'no otherwise qualified individual with a disability in the United States, as defined in section 705(20) of this title, shall, solely by reason of her or his disability, be excluded from the participation in, be denied the benefits of, or be subjected to discrimination under any program or activity receiving federal financial assistance'. In essence, this provision prohibited any programme or activity receiving federal funding from discriminating against a Disabled person. Despite its importance, there was a delay in implementing Section 504 after its passage. New regulations were needed to determine who counted as a Disabled person and what was considered discrimination. These regulations would prevent judges from having to interpret the law for themselves. In one notable case, a wheelchair user attempted to exercise their right to use the public bus system, only to be denied access by a judge's ruling. The judge argued that because the bus driver had stopped and opened the doors, it couldn't have been a case of discrimination, even though the individual was unable to board the bus. Meanwhile, the Department of Health, Education and Welfare, which was responsible for implementing the regulations, made little progress in the years that followed. It wasn't until 1977, the Department of Health, Education and Welfare finally released the proposed regulations, following intense pressure from various stakeholders. However, just as the process was gaining momentum, it was disrupted by a presidential election, causing a change in government that led to a delay. Once the new administration, led by President Jimmy Carter, took office, a task force was established to weaken the regulations. Although it was not explicitly stated on the invitations, it is clear that the task force lacked representation from the disabled community. Notably, President Carter had campaigned on a platform that included supporting the regulations, but significant pressure from affected agencies and universities ultimately influenced the outcome. As the coalition of Disabled people's organisations, which had battled tirelessly to reach this milestone, was assured that the proposed changes were entirely superficial, they sensed that their long-awaited civil rights legislation was being undermined from within. Frustrated by this perceived betrayal, they chose not to wait for the draft regulations to be published. Instead, they issued an ultimatum determined to force the administration to act. If the Department of Health, Education and Welfare failed to issue the unchanged regulations by 4 April 1977, Disabled groups had threatened to stage sit-ins at the department's offices across the country on 5 April. However, it was not surprising that no progress was made on the regulations. Instead, Joseph Califano prepared contingency plans to swiftly address the threatened sit-in. Despite this, the sit-in proceeded. Disabled individuals from all over the country occupied government offices in Atlanta, Boston, Chicago, Denver, Los Angeles, New York, Philadelphia, and Seattle. The most notable protests took place in San Francisco and Washington DC. In California, a committee had been preparing for weeks to hold a rally outside the San Francisco office of the Department of Health, Education and Welfare, but their ultimate plan was to occupy the building for an extended period of time. They spent months beforehand organising speakers, medics, fundraising, publicity, and the logistical arrangements necessary for their prolonged occupation. Following the rally, they entered the building and refused to leave. This occupation, which lasted the longest and became the most prominent protest, ultimately prompted a change of heart in the government. As one of the participants recalled, 'Once we got inside the building, one of the things that was neat was that… this initial structure of… the medics, and the food, and outreach volunteers…this framework remained largely intact, allowing the same committees to continue functioning, but with a much larger team. As a result, most people had something meaningful to contribute.' While other figures from the sit-in may have gained more widespread recognition in contemporary Disability history due to their association with the Crip Camp film, which was produced after Kitty's passing, Cone was the key strategist behind the protest, earning her the reputation as the 'organisational brains' behind the sit-in. According to accounts, she was deeply committed to the idea that 'the broader you build something, the better the chance you have of success,' a conviction that guided her approach to the protest. With this strategy in mind, Cone played a crucial role in mobilising a coalition of supporters from other activist groups that were active at the time. The Black Panthers, for example, supplied food, while the Machinist Union workers provided transportation.

Additionally, supportive politicians sent essential items such as mattresses and temporary showers. According to reports, these organisations held support rallies outside the building, which created a broad and deep level of support that made it increasingly difficult for authorities to take action against the protesters. Despite the impressive display of solidarity outside, the conditions inside the building were reported to be physically gruelling. The utilities had been switched off to force the protestors out, and many individuals with disabilities were separated from their medical and assistive equipment. Despite these challenges, fellow protestors and a few non-disabled personal assistants worked tirelessly to provide personal care to as many individuals as possible. Miraculously, the coordination and organisational skills of those in charge ensured that the situation did not descend into chaos. All decisions that affected those inside the building were made through a democratic process at daily meetings, where everyone was in attendance.

When the government finally relented and decided to engage with the protesters, they held a Congressional hearing inside the San Francisco building. Instead of sending Secretary Califano himself, a low-ranking representative from the Department of Health, Education and Welfare was sent to meet the protestors. This decision did little to alleviate tensions, as the representative's appearance only antagonised the protesters. The situation took a dramatic turn for the worse when he was presented with testimony from individuals with disabilities about their experiences of discrimination. The testimony was so compelling that the representative became overwhelmed, and he ultimately retreated to an office, locking himself inside. In a bold display of support, a Congressman who had attended the meeting had to chase after him and break down the door to coax him out and make him face the protestors. After two weeks of non-stop activism, a small group of protestors was chosen to travel to Washington DC to raise awareness and push for their demands, while the others continued the occupation. The travelling protesters met with members of Congress who had previously supported the administration, but now expressed a desire to address important issues. In front of national TV cameras, the group presented the harsh realities of the situation, methodically refuting each supposed 'issue' raised by the administration's supporters. They did so by systematically addressing each objection, ultimately dismantling the criticisms and highlighting the flaws in the original bill. The demonstrators leveraged the Carter government's election pledge to be open and accessible, using it to their advantage, by strategically targeting their protests and rallies locations where the President and the Secretary of Health, Education and Welfare would be conducting their daily activities. This tactic forced the government officials to use back doors rather than face the protestors directly, which ultimately led to a meeting at the White House, as well as widespread support from individuals who were frustrated by the reluctance to engage with the campaigners. Finally, after an endless stream of pressure from activists, politicians, and the public, on 28 April 1977, Secretary Califano signed the regulations. For the first time in history, people with disabilities in America gained concrete federal civil rights protections. Kitty reflected on this momentous achievement, stating that, 'we had shown ourselves and the country through network television that we, the most hidden, impoverished, and pitied group of people in the nation, were capable of waging a serious struggle that brought about profound social change.' Contrary to many depictions of people with disabilities, the eyes of the nation had been on the individuals participating in the sit-in and then the contingent in Washington, resulting in extensive national news coverage. For the first time, Disability was viewed as a civil rights matter rather than a charity or rehabilitation issue, or at best, a matter of pity. As the excitement and adrenaline from the sit-in wound down, Kitty returned home to her long-term partner Kathy Martinez. Kathy, a blind woman, formed a strong bond with Kitty over Disability politics, and soon became her romantic partner. The Martinez family became something of a surrogate family for Kitty, who had little contact with the few remaining members of her own family. Kathy often said that 'in many ways, our disabilities complemented each other, as she could help Kitty with physical tasks and [Kitty] could help her with visual tasks.' Living in Berkeley, the centre of Disability activism, they were able to overcome many practical barriers by using a bit of ingenuity and playfulness. Kathy fondly remembered many instances where she would put on roller skates and Kitty, in her wheelchair, would pull her around town, effortlessly navigating the streets of Berkeley. Kathy laughed, 'We were quite the iconic pair, able to speed around the city much faster than I could have walked.' She added, 'If proof were needed, it's clear the Paralympics should innovate more.' Despite their frustration with the laws of the time, which forbade same-sex marriage, Kathy and Kitty longed to start a family. After encountering significant obstacles in their adoption attempts in the United States, Kathy and Kitty discovered that their combined circumstances as a gay and disabled couple created an insurmountable amount of bureaucratic red tape. In 1981, Kitty relocated to Mexico, followed closely by Kathy who was inspired by left-wing politics that spoke of Mexico as being a haven for individuals sharing their political beliefs, and her own experiences travelling around South America during her younger years. Kathy believed that Mexico would be the ideal location to grow their family. She had previously spent a year living in a Mexican town with a former girlfriend, during which time she had developed a circle of friends and enjoyed a lively social life, complete with drinking and partying. It was a welcome hiatus from her political and Disability activism. Their knowledge of Mexico proved to be a significant advantage in their adoption journey. A legal loophole, designed to facilitate the relocation of children adopted by American diplomats and government officials, allowed individuals who had lived there for two years or more to bring their adopted child to the United States on a family visa, rather than an adoption visa. Thanks to this opportunity, Kitty and Kathy soon returned to the United States with their son, Jorge. They moved back to California, where Kitty continued her activism work at the World Institute on Disability and the Disability Rights Education and Defense Fund. The Disability Rights Education Defense Fund (DREDF) had evolved from the principles and experiences of the Center for Independent Living in Berkeley, California. As the legal defence fund for Disability-related cases, DREDF played a crucial role in advocating for the rights of individuals with disabilities. In a later reflection, Kitty said: 'don't have any doubt that we would not have the ADA the way we have it today were it not for DREDF, both in terms of mobilising people in the community and educating them.' The finances necessary to fight court cases became vitally important as it had become clear soon after Section 504 was signed that the fight to retain the civil rights introduced by the Rehabilitation Act would be as important as the fight to create them in the first place. Despite the consistent attempts by government and organisations to weaken the regulations, they continued to face resistance from various stakeholders. The aim was to reduce the burden on businesses and government departments, but the momentum was short-lived. Word spread quickly, and it wasn't long before many of the Disabled campaigners who had played a crucial role in securing these civil rights gathered together once again to ensure that they remained unchanged. Public transportation, including buses and trains, proved to be a significant obstacle in implementation of these regulations, requiring a substantial amount of Kitty's time and energy. As her peers sent her to Washington DC to advocate for the rights of Disabled individuals by lobbying individuals and meeting with government officials, the White House was inundated with letters from Disabled people and their families, emphatically protesting any attempts at changing or deregulating section 504.

Throughout the 1980s, the Supreme Court issued a series of rulings that gradually stripped protections for civil rights based on race, gender, and Disability. This necessitated radical action. In response, a coalition of organisations fighting for the civil rights of various groups were formed and formalised, ultimately becoming a crucial factor in the eventual passing of the Americans with Disabilities Act. It was evident from many of the Supreme Court's decisions regarding 504-related litigations that the justices either lacked a comprehensive understanding of section 504 or that excluding someone based on their Disability could be considered as discrimination. In one particular instance, the court admitted that they had not thoroughly considered the guidance issued by the government regarding section 504 when making their decision. This admission was particularly ironic, as the department had been reluctant to issue the regulations in the first place, and the court interpreted this reluctance as evidence that the guidance would not withstand judicial scrutiny. As the judiciary continued to deliver infuriating judgements, it became apparent that the Disabled community would need to take a proactive role in bringing section 504 related cases to court, as well as educating judges on the concept and consequences of Disability discrimination.

The Disability Rights, Education and Defense Fund, led by Kitty, recognised that filing an amicus brief on behalf of sixty-three different Disabled people's organisations would be an effective way to teach the justices and courts about discriminatory employment practices. By including organisations representing both diagnosis-specific and pan-impairment groups, they demonstrated to the courts that this was not a minority issue, but rather a critical concern affecting millions of Americans across the country, with diverse backgrounds and experiences. Following the Supreme Court's exposure to the written advice and the passionate protestations from Disabled individuals across the country, the justices ultimately found that the Health, Education and Welfare regulations and their accompanying guidance, were entitled to great deference by the courts. These original regulations served as the groundwork upon which the later Americans with Disabilities Act would be constructed. The initial draft of the Disability Act was prepared by the National Council on Disability, an independent federal agency created in April 1988 by President Reagan. All members of the council were appointed by Reagan, and as such, the agency was uniquely positioned to provide input on the drafting process. The proposed legislation underwent numerous drafts, revisions, and amendments before its introduction to lawmakers. Despite the complexity of the process, it was clear that the Disabled community would be relentless in their commitment to advocating for the passage of this civil rights legislation. A national campaign was started to ask Disabled people across the country to write their 'discrimination diaries'. These individuals documented their daily experiences as a living testimonial to the grinding afflictions that daily discrimination exacts on everybody. Members of congressional task forces travelled for weeks, zigzagging across the country to hold hearings, gather evidence and document instances of injustices. In September

1988, a full Senate hearing was held. Witnesses with a huge variety of impairments and experiences testified to the senate about the sheer level of exclusion, stereotyping, and prejudice they faced as Disabled individuals. More than 700 people were physically present in person, and the hearing chair made a commitment to everyone in the room who shared their story that a comprehensive disability civil rights bill would be a top priority for lawmakers during the next congressional period. As the hearing took place in the lead-up to an election, both presidential candidates publicly endorsed civil rights protections for individuals with disabilities. Seizing the opportunity, lawmakers scored some easy points, as the work of activists had raised the public's growing awareness of the discrimination faced by people with disabilities. These advocates, however, were not about to let the politicians forget about their campaign promises. Throughout the hearings and the push for public support, the various legal complications of drafting the bill were being worked on by strategists, analysts, lawyers, and politicians in the highest towers of politics. In the meantime, the various Disability organisations involved, organised and rallied their members. Some Disabled individuals and their carers travelled from far away and slept on floors in government buildings so they could testify in congressional hearings. Outside of Washington, a grassroots movement unfolded, with some individuals participating in community responses by mail and telephone to support the cause, while others attended local protests to demand the passing of disability civil rights legislation. As public perception and awareness of the need for legislation to protect Disabled people continued to grow, business leaders outside of government began to recognise the implications of how this bill would affect them. Consequently business owner associations lobbied their members to contact their members of Congress, urging them to oppose or weaken the bill, citing concerns that this legislation would undermine the free market and the economy as a whole.

As the story unfolded, it was only natural to expect unwavering commitment from the Disabled campaigners. They launched a sustained campaign, pestering and inundating lawmakers with a continuous flow of letters, phone calls, and submissions to the committee hearings established to examine the bill. This correspondence storm was enough to overwhelm the deniers. However, the transportation lobby was more vocal and proved more difficult to silence. Greyhound, Amtrak and other national bus and train companies were attempting to convince lawmakers to grant them exemptions from making their vehicles accessible. As a result, the bill had been stalled for months in the committee stages. The ordinary Americans with disabilities had had enough. They demanded their civil rights. In response, they enlisted the support of ADAPT, a prominent advocacy transport campaign group, dedicated to accessible public transportation. ADAPT, which stands for Americans Disabled for Accessible Public Transit, was well known for its unconventional tactics, including traffic-jamming protests. Their speciality was to occupy a public bus, then lie down on the stairs and attempt to crawl up them, illustrating how inaccessible they were. On a spring day in Washington DC, another hearing had taken place. A group of activists and campaigners who had participated in the meeting felt this was the ideal opportunity to put into action an idea they had been considering.

On the morning of 12 March, a group of protesters gathered

outside the White House, accompanied by supporters and banners, and began their march down Pennsylvania Avenue towards the Congress building. As they walked, more people joined the march, until eventually a group of 1,000 people amassed at the bottom of the steps of Congress. The group was treated to speakers and chants, with the crowd asserting that 'access is our right' and threatening that 'we will ride!' Meanwhile, members of ADAPT prepared themselves for their planned action, waiting for their cue. On stage, a speaker held up a small book and addressed the crowd, saying 'the preamble to the Constitution does not say "we the able-bodied people", it says 'we the people.''' This was their code for action. ADAPT members suddenly abandoned their wheelchairs, discarded their crutches, walkers, and canes, and proceeded to attempt to crawl up the seventy-eight steps of the Capitol. Others who hadn't been briefed on the plan, quickly grasped the significance and shed their aids and joined the others. Before long, 60 people from diverse age groups and abilities were dragging themselves up the stairs on their hands and knees. Among them was 8-year-old Jennifer Keelan-Chaffins, who would later become the iconic face of the Capitol Crawl. The next phase of their plan for direct action unfolded in a manner that was impossible to ignore: a guided tour. As planned, 200 Disabled activists arrived for their scheduled appointment to be shown around the building. Despite the large number of people, staff managed to accommodate them all. The activists then chained their wheelchairs together in the middle of the floor, refusing to leave until they were granted an audience with the Republican House leader and the Speaker. When the politicians' responses failed to meet their demands, the protesters refused to disperse. The police were called, and 104 protestors were arrested. However, the federal building's inaccessibility posed a mighty challenge. With only one small lift available, it took the police six hours to remove all of the Disabled individuals from the building. The next step of their action plan was to take their protest directly to the person they held responsible. The next day they entered and occupied the office of the author of the wrecking amendment, which had been lobbied for by the transport companies. As a result of their stunt, the organisers were given a $500 fine and ordered to register for a year's probation. However, when they tried to do so, the federally funded probation office had only a small wooden wheelchair ramp that had rotted away, making it impossible for them to enter the building to register. Eventually their lawyer intervened and registered on their behalf.

One of the major obstacles to the passage of the Americans with Disabilities Act (ADA) was which groups would be included, or rather, which groups could be excluded. From the beginning, impairment-specific and fixed-issue groups vowed to work together to ensure that no-one was left behind in the legislation. This commitment was frequently tested by members of Congress who repeatedly proposed exclusions for individuals with mental illnesses, those with HIV/AIDS, and others. This issue had been a contentious point during the legal fight surrounding the section 504 regulations, specifically those with 'contagious diseases'. In the Supreme Court case that encapsulated this issue, a woman with tuberculosis was the lead. However, it was widely recognised that the court's decision would be vital to protect HIV/AIDS positive individuals from discrimination. At the time, Disabled groups collaborated with lawyers and HIV/AIDs organisations to file and present legal information about HIV and AIDs. This collective effort resulted in the creation of connections that would be vital during the arduous process of passing the Americans with Disabilities Act (ADA). As the bill neared its final passage, most of the contentious issues had been resolved. However, a last-minute amendment known as the Chapman amendment, was filed, seeking to exclude individuals with AIDs or other contagious diseases who worked in the food industry from protection against discrimination. Despite this new development, the Disability groups involved in the negotiations remained steadfast in their commitment to ensure that no group would be discriminated against. In accordance with their earlier promise, they refused to accept any changes that would perpetuate discrimination against individuals with certain impairments or specific issues. It is widely acknowledged that this stance could have indefinitely postponed or even lost the bill. Nevertheless, the Disabled community stood united in their conviction that anti-discrimination legislation was nothing if it didn't provide protection for everyone.

The bill's progress continued, with votes following emotionally charged hearings in the Senate where people shared emotional stories of their personal experiences with discrimination. As the hearings concluded, members of Congress began to understand the levels of unfairness, the devastating effects of intolerance, and the need for a comprehensive law for all Disabled Americans.

The journey was long and tedious, requiring many Disabled activists to pivot to working with politicians. This transition was particularly challenging and the sudden shift from adversary to collaborator required a significant adjustment. On a sunny yet breezy day outside the White House on 26 July 1990, George H.W. Bush hosted a ceremony on the South Lawn. Sharing the podium with two wheelchair users, an armless minister, a parent campaigner, and a sign language interpreter, Bush sat down at a desk and signed the Americans with Disabilities Act into law. The ceremony was watched by hundreds of fellow campaigners who had tirelessly fought for the legislation, which was hailed by many as the world's first comprehensive civil rights law for people with disabilities. Naturally, this wasn't the end. If we've learned anything, it is this stark reality, that some individuals will continue to resist the notion of equal treatment. Despite the numerous amendments made to this legislation over the years, and the numerous attempts by many companies, organisations, and individuals to challenge these laws in the Supreme Court, it is crucial to recognise that many of those involved in the passage of the Americans with Disabilities Act were also seasoned advocates from the section 504 campaigns. As expected, they were well prepared for the legal challenges that would arise. The organisation where Kitty Cone worked immediately began preparing for the impending legal challenges. DREDF played a crucial role in this effort, writing amicus briefs on behalf of members of Congress or representing disability groups. In one case, they co-counselled alongside the NAACP Legal Defense Fund before the Supreme Court, ultimately shaping the Court's understanding of disability as a civil rights issue. The Sutton Trilogy and Olmstead vs LC cases are two examples of challenges to the Americans with Disabilities Act, which narrowed the definition of disability by excluding individuals who use 'mitigating measures' such as medication to alleviate impairments. Olmstead vs LC recognised what most Disabled people had known for decades, that, 'unjustified institutional isolation of persons with disabilities is a form of discrimination'.

Although Kitty Cone eventually retired, she never fully gave up her commitment to activism, which had become an integral part of who she was. Her experiences with disability had profoundly impacted every aspect of her life. 'My entire history, everything in my life, from where I live, to who my child is, to the people I know and love – everything, my entire course in life was profoundly affected by having a disability,' she said. 'The school, the university I went to, the fact that I moved to the Bay Area because of its good climate – it all had to do with my disability. So I am thankful for my disability. I feel like the constraints and the choices that it has given me have made me who I am, and you know, I like who I am.'

Connie Panzarino

'Trached dykes eat pussy without coming up for air'

Not everyone finds it easy to like themselves. For many individuals, self-acceptance and self-liking is not a naturally occurring phenomenon. Growing up with feelings of shame that arise from hearing the subtle, and sometimes not so subtle, comments from those around you about the things you can't change is difficult to cast off. Regardless of whether someone is Queer, Disabled, or faces another marginalised identity, the underlying sentiment is unmistakable: the assumption that everything would be better if one were not afflicted with a disability. This pervasive notion that everything would be better by erasing one's differences is a constant notion that can be hard to shake. To the contrary, when Connie Panzarino realised that she felt proud of her identity, she decided she wanted to try and make sure everyone else felt that way too.

Connie Panzarino was born in New York City in November 1947, she was raised on Long Island with her parents. All seemed fine when she was a baby and her parents doted on her. But as she grew into a toddler, it became clear that something wasn't quite right. As a young child, Connie's development slowed. Despite her parents' concerns, doctors repeatedly dismissed them, attributing her struggles to laziness, exaggeration or imagination. Her parents sensed that something was fundamentally wrong. It wasn't until much later in Connie's life that she would be diagnosed with Werdnig-Hoffmann disease, a degenerative neuromuscular condition, also known as spinal muscular atrophy type III. Connie's childhood was marked by a series of visits to various doctors, accompanied by her parents. The hospital became a familiar and unsettling environment, where she spent weeks undergoing a series of tests. It was during this time that she first used a wheelchair, and the freedom it brought her was a revelation. When she was discharged, Connie was devastated to leave it behind. She was given the diagnosis of amyotonia congenita. It was a broad estimate, more than a definitive diagnosis. During this period it was an umbrella term for 'a congenital muscle tone disorder'. It was a close guess, but a guess all the same. It wasn't until her younger sister was born with the same condition that Connie began to realise the truth. The comparison between the sister's abilities made it clear that she really couldn't walk, and not simply lacking motivation, but a genuine impairment. Connie watched other children grow up and attend school, from which she'd been prohibited because they felt unable to confidently lift her on and off the toilet. For years, teachers sporadically visited her home, usually only for a single hour once a day. They would drop off a day's worth of homework and leave her to it. After a while, an intercom system allowed Connie to be part of the same classes but she found it impossible to follow the lessons without being able to see the blackboard, and quickly lost interest.

At the age of eleven, Connie was made the poster child for the Long Island Muscular Dystrophy Association fundraising campaign. She was deeply confused and asked her mother, 'But I don't have muscular dystrophy, do I?' Her mother said, 'no', adding further perplexity to the situation. Apparently, the view from the Muscular Dystrophy Association was that 'being a poster child makes many of the kids with muscular dystrophy too tired and sometimes they die sooner from the stress'. Despite the concerns of being a poster child, the Muscular Dystrophy Association didn't reconsider their approach, but instead decided that the best way around this was to recruit children with vaguely similar diseases to be on their banners. This unexpected offer did, however, give Connie opportunities she may not have had. As she travelled the country, meeting many famous people and learning about the media and how to present herself to the public, she said, 'I learned how to smile and speak clearly. They taught me how to position my body to look appealing yet evoke compassion. I learned to open my eyes wider for the camera so that I look more pleading.' After years of struggling to attend school, Connie finally made a breakthrough in the 7th grade. She was able to suppress her need to use the bathroom which made it possible for her to attend school for half a day at a time. It soon became obvious that many of the families in the area with Disabled children had been complaining about the appalling home school options available for their children. The school administration noted Connie's success and promised to consider allowing other Disabled children to attend if they didn't need to use the toilet. By the end of that year, Connie's 'good urinary behaviour' allowed her the right to stay an extra lesson longer, and more Disabled children were allowed to start at the school. Connie made many friends at school, but was also exposed to unpleasant attitudes of others for the first time. One friend's mother prohibited her daughter from pushing Connie around the school in her wheelchair, raising concerns about being at risk of being sued for any injuries.

Many others seemed to assume that Connie's dreams and desires were limited, failing to see her as any other young girl her age. But when Connie turned 14, she received a phone call and was invited to meet with a group of other disabled teenagers. Connie knew some of these individuals from a few Disabled summer camps she'd attended, specifically designed for Disabled youth, where they were able to freely connect and share stories without the attitudes of others encumbering them. At the camp, many of the non-disabled volunteers were a similar age to the campers, and there was very little distinction between the two groups. They went to the same parties and became friends. But when a disabled participant and non-disabled volunteer started dating, the dynamics shifted. Connie doesn't mention the name of this summer camp in her book, but given it's likeness to a less restrictive camp for Disabled youth in New York State, it could well be Camp Jened, the famous Crip Camp.

This meeting with disabled young adults turned into a club, where they could raise money to fund outings and trips and learn about their rights and how they could best fight for what they deserved and what they were entitled to. The club arranged for speakers, went on trips, and heard from other disabled individuals who had been affected by the issues they were concerned with. They formed committees to learn about employment and social security benefits. However, amidst these empowering experiences, Connie faced a harsh reality: many of her friends with life-limiting illnesses were dying, making her acutely aware of her own existence. Around this time, Connie's family moved to a different suburb hoping to find a more accessible environment for the children. While this move offered benefits, it further isolated Connie from her friends, leaving her very lonely and afraid about the possibility of never seeing them again. However, the young adults' group provided Connie with a chance for effecting real change. The group's efforts to open a brand-new library near the family's new home was wonderful but she was frustrated to find that it wasn't accessible. Connie decided that this was an opportunity to create a nuisance to prove a point. Connie phoned them and politely asked if she could attend their next board meeting to speak about accessibility. She made it clear that since there was no ramp, the board would have to carry wheelchair users up and down the stairs. Sensing an excellent photo opportunity, Connie called the five biggest wheelchair users and the local newspaper. When she arrived at the library, she pretnded to look surprised as eight middle-aged men in suits struggled to carry adult wheelchair users down the stairs into the basement meeting room. The scene was so striking that the board immediately voted to build a ramp to make the library accessible for all.

As Connie's high school graduation in 1965 approached, she had undergone a series of academic tests from the Office of Vocational Rehabilitation to determine whether they would fund her university studies. After some toing and froing, they agreed to let her study English, provided she chose the right programme. However, Connie's first application to the state university was rejected because while it was architecturally accessible, their misguided decision was that 'a Disabled person couldn't really expect to go to college'. She was, however, admitted to Hofstra University, even though it was inaccessible to wheelchair users. Hofstra was one of only two universities that admitted disabled students. One of her professors, a disabled individual himself, made a profound impact on Connie. He spoke of autonomy and civil rights, and sparked a passion within her. While at college, she finally felt a sense of freedom and although she had to return to her family's home at the end of every day, she had time to herself, where her parents and teachers didn't know where she was or what she was doing. During this time, Connie joined a sorority, went to parties, and studied, and started a group for people who supported the rights and inclusion of disabled students. They called it People United in Support of the Handicapped, or 'PUSH' for short. Unlike the young adults' group she had been a part of, this one was designed to include both Disabled and non-disabled people, and eventually came to represent the Disabled students across the university. Their advocacy efforts took them to Washington DC, where they lobbied for Disabled students and their future employment rights. On campus, PUSH worked with the university to campaign for an accessible campus and inclusivity.

One of their most thrilling initiatives was challenging the most famous basketball team in the world, the Harlem Globetrotters, to play them in chairs. The challenge was accepted, and the game was televised as a fundraising event. After graduating from college, Connie struggled to find a job that matched her passions and skills. The editing and writing jobs she was interested in were either located in inaccessible locations, or had no interest in hiring a Disabled person, and so she returned to the university, to volunteer in the Disabled student's organisation that she had set up and worked part time as a research assistant for one of her professors. It was then that Connie met Ron Kovic again after many years apart. They had attended the same high school but hadn't seen each other since graduation. In the time between their meetings, he had fought in the Vietnam War and had suffered a life-altering injury, returning to the US with no use of his legs and PTSD. They began dating and had a relationship that lasted many years with mixed levels of success and happiness. However, despite the challenges they faced, Connie and Ron managed to significantly broaden each other's worlds and they both became political activists. Ron, in particular, was moved by Connie's continued support, saying 'she stood by me like no one else, listened through nights and days, caring and loving, understanding and encouraging, wiping the tears from my eyes.' Meanwhile, Connie continued to search for more suitable work to support herself. She was refused disability benefits because she was able to work, but she was also refused a job by everyone else on the basis that she was disabled. After another infuriating meeting with the social security office, Connie's frustration reached a tipping point. Connie stormed down the corridor of the social security office and demanded a job there, since they were the ones making these strange rules. Surprisingly, her bold demand worked, and she worked there for many years. Finally financially independent, she moved out of home, and into her own apartment with her friend Priscilla, who had previously been living in a care home for the elderly. As Connie's frustration with the government's policies increased, she became disillusioned. She felt the injustices against herself and regular people personally. Connie's major issue was the need for a personal assistant. It was unreasonable to expect her parents to assume responsibility of caring for her and her sister. Finally, in their own home, Priscilla's financial independence allowed her to hire her own care assistants and Connie could make her own choices. Given this freedom, Connie was able to pursue her own interests, including visiting Ron and his friends when they campaigned against the government's treatment of Vietnam veterans. However, this independence presented its own challenges. While Connie was away with Ron, he could help with her care needs, but when she returned to the apartment, she was entirely alone. Connie needed to pay for attendant care, but she was unable to receive the social security benefits needed to pay for attendant care. The government said that legally, since she was able to work, she was not technically Disabled.

To Connie, and many others, this was ridiculous and absurd. The idea that having a job meant she no longer needed attendant care was laughable, and she wasn't making enough money to pay for it because her social security salary was so meagre. She called her local government contacts to find a way around this rule, and they were as surprised as she was by this loophole, but they couldn't find a solution. The only way to change this nonsensical legislation was by amending the Medicaid laws. The health secretary himself was baffled by this situation and couldn't find a solution either. Connie was forced to relinquish her job to apply for disability benefits, a devastating decision that allowed her to access the attendant care she needed to survive. She felt disillusioned by the challenging situation, 'Society is saying to me, "be an invalid."' Undeterred, Connie spent months tirelessly campaigning, appearing in newspapers, on TV, and speaking to politicians. She worked with her Congressman to write a bill allowing Disabled people to work without losing their disability status. Though the original bill was killed off at the last minute, Connie persevered. She went back and forth to Congress many times during 1977, first to campaign for the introduction of Section 504 of the Rehabilitation Act, and secondly for this. She wrote a letter to fellow Disabled people called, 'there is no such thing as disabled worker'. She explained that 'we are costing the Government twice as much as we should, and we are not being allowed to contribute to our society'.

Within one year she had helped write eleven different local, state level and national level bills to change this discrepancy.

During this time, she had moved to California, partly because she liked the idea of the warmer climate, but also because she had heard that in California Disabled people were allowed to work and get disability benefits. In addition, Ron had suddenly upped and moved too. Their relationship however was troubled. He had relationships with other women and encouraged her to seek out sexual experiences with other men, and women. She wasn't interested in the idea of having sex with other people, although she was intrigued by the prospect of relationships with women. Soon after Connie was allowed to work and get benefits back in her home state, they moved back to New York with the intention of Connie pursuing an art therapy degree. They moved into their own apartment together, although he would often go away for months at a time without telling her where he was or how long he would be gone for.

In preparation for her return to studying, she took a lot of short courses and one of them, on sexuality, really caught her attention. She realised that many of her early crushes had been on women. She and Ron broke up, and she almost immediately realised that she didn't mind all that much, because she was in love with her attendant. Her feelings were so strong that they almost stopped her breathing, and required her to crank up the settings on her ventilator. This realisation, and their brief relationship, allowed Connie to understand things about herself and her body that she had never experienced before but unfortunately, it opened her eyes to how she was viewed as a Disabled woman in the lesbian community.

She began writing poetry and won prizes at open mic nights. She became deeply frustrated with the amount of ableism in the Queer community. She overheard people talk about why anyone would date her when there were other non-Disabled lesbians available. The paternalism that exists around disability means many people wouldn't consider that someone could be sexual at all, let alone be gay. Connie once had a straight attendant that assumed she was gay only because she couldn't find a suitable man, and refused to march in the Gay Pride

Parade with her because she was afraid other people might think she was a lesbian. It was a big deal when Connie decided to march in the Gay Pride Parade. While her brother and sister knew she was gay, her parents didn't, so her brother unplugged all the televisions in the house so that her parents wouldn't see her on the news. Soon Connie joined a community of other Disabled lesbians and formed a group with them. They began hosting workshops and sessions with different types of people, teaching them about the oppression of Disabled people, Queer people, and those who were both.

It's widely accepted that there are often significantly worse outcomes in healthcare for LGBTQ+ individuals. Whether that's not getting the test that's needed because someone assumes you're not at risk or someone actively refusing to treat you because you're Queer. This is also the case in care facilities, where people are forced to hide their true selves or face discrimination from the people they rely on for healthcare. While it's been prevalent for many decades, it has started to get more attention as the older members of the gay rights movement are moving into residential care facilities. In care homes, vicars, priests and pastors are often visiting for end-of-life care, and sometimes residents are reportedly cajoled into talking to them to 'repent their sins'. Many have experienced homophobic assaults, and others have had carers refuse to visit their homes because they disapprove of the things in the house.

Connie mostly avoided this problem by hiring predominantly Queer personal assistants, but that didn't mean she didn't have to campaign at all anymore. Going back to education and having less time for the bar and her poetry didn't stop her activism though. While living in the accessible dorms at New York

University, the administration decided that they weren't going to be able to install the wheelchair accessible showers when they said they would and couldn't tell anyone when they were likely to be able to use them. So Connie arranged a shower strike. In a stroke of unrivalled and terrifying genius, she called on her fellow students to refuse to shower until their Disabled peers were able to, saying that 'together we could raise a stench that would rock the administration into action'. I expect based on the strength of that threat and less because 'they wanted to do the right thing', less than a week after the call to armpits was published in the student newspaper, the university relented and allowed the students to wash.

Connie received a call from someone she knew who was looking to sell their farmhouse in upstate New York. Connie used all of her savings to buy it and turned it into a commune for disabled lesbians. They all split chores and tasks evenly and encouraged collective care, as well as collectively working to unlearn their own internalised ableism and homophobia. In time her muscle function began to diminish and she couldn't move freely. With trepidation she went to a rehab hospital to learn to use equipment that would help her with her limited mobility. After graduating with her Master's in art therapy, she moved to Boston and began working as the director of the Boston Self Help Center. As a licensed art therapist, Connie also took on private clients. In her free time, Connie used her evenings and weekends to give talks on sexism, homophobia, and ableism, as well as working with abuse survivors. But before long, her services as a Disability campaigner were required, and she was hired as the director of the Boston Center for Independent Living. There she met Catherine Odette who was the publisher of the magazine *Dykes, Disability & Stuff*, along with her partner Sara Karon. It was a magazine made up of reviews, articles, news of issues of interest to Queer Disabled women and reader submissions including letters, poetry and art. The magazine created 'a communications network for disabled dykes . . . to help build a strong lesbian community,' amongst those hidden and not necessarily seen outside of the assumed narrative of gay women. Catherine and Sara were living in Boston at this time, and they, along with Disabled People's Organisations in the area, such as the Boston Center for Independent Living, decided to push back against the biases, stereotypes and negative connotations of Disability in a very public way by forming the Disability Pride Day Coalition.

They saw how the theories and concepts of Gay Pride and Black Pride had allowed people to celebrate their identity that had previously been made to feel ashamed about. The intention of the original Disability Pride Day was to celebrate the passing of the landmark Americans with Disabilities Act and commemorate the work of the Disability Rights movement, the work against ableism within society and to raise awareness of the social model of disability. The first ever Disability Pride Parade in Boston on 6 October 1990 garnered far more attention than anyone expected. 'More than 400 people marched, drove, wheeled and moved from City Hall to Boston Common in a demonstration to affirm that, "far from tragic, disability is a natural part of the human experience."' It was a huge success with Karen Thompson (partner of Sharon Kowalski, featured in the next chapter) as the guest speaker who rallied the crowd around the message of Disability inclusion and equality. A second event was planned for the year after, but unfortunately when Catherine and Sara moved away from Boston, and another lead organiser died, it was cancelled. While the idea of Disability Pride lingered on in people's minds, it wasn't until 2004 in Chicago that another Disability Pride Parade was held in the United States. It has run every year since (aside from a break for the Covid 19 pandemic) and has only become popular and more widely known. New York City held several Disability Independence Day events between 1992 and 1996. To mark the 25th anniversary of the signing of the Americans with Disabilities Act, the Mayor of New York at the time, Bill Di Blasio, declared the whole month of July as Disability Pride Month. They celebrated with a new Disability Pride Parade, and the rest of the country and world joined in, even creating a flag to represent the Disability pride movement.

Connie left an incredible legacy, and few people know the history of the Disability Pride movement, and very few people know why they now have the option to have a job even if they need personal care. Her legacy in activism and legislation, much of her poetry and academic work is still considered by those studying and researching intersectional Queer and Disability studies to this day.

Connie spent most of her life arguing with people about her rights. She knew this made life difficult for other people. She dedicated much of her life to campaigning for accessibility and the rights of her and her friends. The legacy of her activism and work with Disability Pride will long continue.

Sharon Kowalski & Karen Thompson

'Sharon chose her family, but the judge didn't agree'

People often speak of a campaigner's commitment to changing the world for the better, but in the case of most people, few set out to become activists. Activism became a part of their lives as they sought the support and understanding they deserved for the injustices they face. This was the case for Sharon Kowalski and her partner Karen.

Sharon's life in St Cloud, Minnesota had been simple, happy and most of all, normal. She was a highly respected and well-liked PE and Health teacher at a local high school, and had lived with her partner, Karen Thompson, a lecturer at a nearby college, for four years. While Sharon's parents were unaware of the romantic nature of their relationship, 13 November 1983 seemed like a normal day as Sharon drove through town, a routine followed countless times. Suddenly, another car ploughed into her, driven by a drunk driver. She was seriously injured, and after many months in hospital, and numerous attempts at rehabilitation, she was discharged to a nursing home with significant brain damage and the alleged mental capability of a toddler. As a result of her injuries, her immediate friends felt she needed someone to take responsibility for her care. One day, a judge received a contested application for guardianship. Guardianship is a process where the court appoints someone to make medical and financial decisions on behalf of the person who is considered unable to make those choices. In March 1984, both Sharon's partner, Karen and Sharon's parents petitioned for guardianship.

The use of legal schemes and procedures to remove rights from Disabled people deemed 'unable to decide for themselves' has a long history. In Roman times the head of the household, the 'pater familias', was given ultimate power over those who were vulnerable or mentally incapable of making their own decisions. This often included children, women, and slaves, as well as those with cognitive impairments and learning disabilities. Guardianships as a legal entity are said to have emerged in England in 1660, although it's accepted that these kinds of arrangements had existed informally for much longer. For instance, Massachusetts, an early English colony that adopted many English laws, had a guardianship law on its books from 1641. In the twentieth century, many people who were committed under guardianship orders would have been people we wouldn't consider incapable of decision making, they were labelled 'deviants', but we would just call them a little eccentric. The state law allowed someone to either be declared the guardian of the personal decisions or the financial decisions of the individual, although in 80 per cent of cases it was both. These guardianships were granted on one of three grounds: if someone was a 'minor', 'insane' or 'mentally incompetent'. There was very little ongoing supervision of these orders, unless the guardian was trying to sell property that belonged to the guarded individual. Regarding that specific issue, the courts were unusually meticulous and particular. Most of the guardianships filed during this time period were for minors, with the mother appointed the guardian. Legally, a father was automatically the guardian of a child and it only reverted to the mother if the couple had been married, and the father died. Even then, it was only 'while she remains unmarried', and in most cases, the only safe option to care for their children's affairs was to petition the court to become their legal guardian. One phenomenal record sits in the California casebooks from 19 June 1900, where Horance Philbrook, an ex-lawyer who was banned from practising law due to questionable ethics, tried to file for guardianship of a man named James Merrit. He claimed Merrit was legally incompetent, but as later discovered, Merrit also happened to be the heir to a $2.2 million fortune left by his mother. It was rare for guardianship petitions to be denied. Not only was it refused, Philbrook was charged with extortion. These orders controlled and limited Disabled people. In Oklahoma, there are records of Native Americans being put under spurious guardianships due to alleged 'incompetency', justified on the grounds that they didn't write in perfect English.

These guardianships gave the authority to control, farm, use and lease out their land without having to request permission from, or even talk to the landowners themselves. This contributes to the mounting evidence showing the unsettling and undeniable history of exploitation, and further marginalisation of minority communities, a disturbing trend that continues within most existing systems to this day.

Legal protection for vulnerable people has been an essential tool for fighting exploitation for hundreds of years. In most countries throughout the world, Disabled people are made 'wards of the court'. These judgements are decided upon by a single judge and are often based on patronising and paternalistic assumptions about the mental capacity of Disabled people, particularly those with certain intellectual, learning or cognitive disabilities. These orders transfer the rights of Disabled people from themselves to a third party; while they are intended to protect the individual in question they are actually ripe for exploitation and are considered a form of 'civil death'. This type of proscriptive mandate is a last resort and the courts technically require someone to act in a person's best interests. Currently, there are few ongoing checks ensuring that guardians adhere to their responsibilities or that decisions for the individual continue to be 'in someone's best interests'. Leading up to late 2021, Britney Spears' conservatorship case raised the profile of guardianships and similar court orders imposed on Disabled people. She told the court how she had been forced to work on projects whether she wanted to or not, had not been prohibited from getting married and had been barred from removing a contraceptive IUD allowing her to fall pregnant again. It seemed outrageous that someone who could clearly and plainly articulated their opinions and preferences would be sealed into a legal guardianship order. For many Disabled people though, this wasn't a surprise but a vindication of several campaigns that had been rumbling through the courts. Primarily, the people forced into these kinds of guardianship or conservator arrangements have learning disabilities, cognitive impairments or have acquired brain injuries. They are believed or assumed to be unable to adequately communicate, but alleged unstable mental illness has also been used as a justification to permanently remove someone's rights.

These orders regularly remove the recipient's right to oversee major decisions in their lives, such as where they live, what medical treatment they want, need, and receive and how to spend their money. The inevitable result is a power imbalance between the ward and their legal guardian. Ward are left unable to make any decisions for themselves, even minor, inconsequential decisions on the basis that it's 'for their own good'. The Convention on the Rights of Persons with Disabilities by the United Nations in 2006 protects the right for those with learning disabilities or intellectual impairments to have 'the support they may require' to make decisions for themselves. Since the adoption of this convention by 182 countries, several governments have reformed their guardianship processes to consider the opinions and decisions of the Disabled people themselves, and to restrict the influence of stigmas and individual biases. The success of this though is inevitably debatable.

When both Sharon Kowalski's parents and Karen Thompson applied in the courts to be appointed her guardian, the two parties came to a compromise. Karen wanted Sharon to return home to be cared for by herself and a series of home nurses where she would be amongst her friends. Sharon's parents, however, wanted Sharon to be sent to a nursing home. Karen eventually agreed that Donald Kowalski could be awarded guardianship, on the condition that she would have both the legal right and the family's permission to regularly visit whichever facility Sharon lived in. However, when the Kowalskis found out about the true nature of Karen and Sharon's relationship, they changed their minds. They negated their original agreement and moved Sharon to a nursing home a five-hour drive away, and banned Karen from visiting. Thompson attempted to appeal this demand that the legally binding agreement had been ignored. The court heard testimony from Sharon's parents as they defended their refusal to allow Karen to visit by claiming that the healthcare workers had advised them that Sharon became agitated and upset when Karen had to leave. Therefore, to spare her, it would be better if Karen was prevented from visiting. This view of 'upset' as being an emotion to be prevented by legal guardians, ignoring any of the norms of human behaviour was considered enough to deprive someone of their liberty.

This phenomenon included anyone who held a position of authority, even outside the rules of guardianship. In the case of HL in the UK, this meant life changing decisions had been taken out of his hands and given to named and trusted legal guardians. These rights were taken with no opportunity for either the ward or the guardians to express a view. In this situation, an extreme power imbalance meant that medics decided that they knew best and were able to take control. Despite HL's learning disabilities and having been considered incapable of consenting to medical treatment, he had been living in the community with paid adult foster carers, who took responsibility for his medical and financial decisions. He had been institutionalised for nearly thirty years, and his community care was still handled by the hospital he had been kept in. While at a day centre, he had become 'upset and agitated', and as a result was sedated and admitted to the emergency department of the hospital. Based on the claim that his behaviour showed he was at risk of harming himself or others, he was held for five months against the wishes of his guardians, before eventually being discharged into their care in December 1997. Since he was considered 'informally detained' and wasn't being forced to stay, he should have been free to leave whenever his court appointed guardians requested. Even though he was not being officially detained and could legally leave whenever he wanted, the hospital prevented his carers from visiting so that they were unable to discharge and leave with him. Hospital staff believed they were 'entitled to treat HL as an in-patient without his consent if he did not dissent', while using his dissent as a reason to hold him. His carers believed, and were convinced he had been falsely imprisoned, and unlawfully detained, and after spending months trying to prove it to the UK courts, the case was discussed in the House of Lords. Here, their opinion was clear; that the hospital's claim he had always been free to go was a 'fairytale'. Eventually at the European Court of Human Rights, a judgement called *HL vs the United Kingdom*, the court declared he had been unlawfully deprived of his liberty. This ruling had widespread consequences for those informally detained in hospitals across the UK. The continued belief from many in the medical profession that a carer fighting for a loved one's wishes is overbearing, disruptive and aggressive usually comes from the assumption that those unable to express their wishes don't have them, and so their carers make an unnecessary fuss. This includes a person's feelings. The idea that a non-verbal person's feelings are only a projection of someone else's emotions leads to situations where all emotions, good and bad, are suppressed for 'the good of the patient', as happened to Sharon.

It was during the first appeal of Sharon Kowalski's guardianship by her partner Karen that Donald Kowalski claimed that 'Karen Thompson kicked herself out of the care home by being aggressive and by driving Sharon into a deep depression'. He said that 'she told Sharon she was being held prisoner, that she was in a dangerous environment. If you couldn't talk and you were lying there, wouldn't that put you into a depression?' Rather than try to help Sharon live with her new circumstances, they petitioned the court to cut all contact with her previous life. He did this by denying that Sharon was a lesbian, and a doctor the family hired wrote to the court to say that 'visits by Karen Thompson at this time would expose Sharon Kowalski to a high risk of sexual abuse' based on no other evidence than his own homophobic prejudice. By this time, several gay rights and civil liberties groups had heard about the case and joined to support Karen in court to not only reclaim her visitation rights, but even acquire guardianship of her partner. This case caught the attention of the gay community because of the fear that many Queer people had was that their estranged relatives, who shunned them for their identities, could be allowed to take over their lives. The idea that someone could prevent them from being part of their communities, choose who was allowed to visit or stop them from seeing their partners and friends was terrifying. Even without the additional element of queerness and the extra dimensions that brings to family relationships, there are numerous and frequent anecdotal accounts of terminal patients expressing their treatment wishes and designating a partner as proxy, only for their parents to turn up and override the patient to demand alternative medical care. This took place in the shadow of the looming AIDs crisis and fed into the real fear that AIDs patients in hospitals would be separated from their partners. This was not a baseless assumption, there was plenty of evidence to prove this was happening. Our knowledge of the numerous campaigns for gay rights is often focussed on the calls for equal marriage and the right to a family and private life. The rights of a same-sex partner to visit their loved one in hospital had not existed for many people for a long time and didn't garner the same level of campaigning that marriage rights and adoption did.

Historically, in the US, individual hospitals had the right to decide who would be allowed to visit patients, and as many hospitals were, and still are, Catholic run, they would restrict visitors from same-sex and unmarried partners. In some states, hospitals would allow visitation for same-sex couples only if a 'traditional' family member or blood relation was not available. There was a push to allow hospital patients to have the legal right to choose who was allowed to visit them, but this was to allow for people without immediate families, and those with 'found families' as it was for gay couples. In 1989, during the AIDs crisis, the gay-friendly city of San Francisco gave queer couples the right to register their same-sex domestic partnerships to gain rights standard for heterosexual couples such as health benefits, hospital visitation rights, and bereavement leave. This was not transferable to other cities in the country, but for the price of $35 a couple could file a 'declaration of domestic partnership' to allow a little peace of mind. For many couples, a partner being granted a medical power of attorney was the only reassurance. This was to ensure their relationship would be considered when making medical or financial decisions, however, it was no guarantee the hospital would abide by the law. This was the unfortunate case for Lisa Pond, who collapsed in Florida in 2007 while on holiday with her partner of twenty years, Janice, and their adopted children. The couple had signed legal papers that agreed Janice would be designated as Lisa's legal guardian if something happened and she required someone to make her decisions for her. But when she was hospitalised with an aneurysm the staff didn't recognise their relationship. A social worker told the family that as Florida was an 'anti-gay' state, they wouldn't be allowed to see Lisa at all. Even though Janice contacted friends at home and had the legally recognised power of attorney paperwork immediately faxed to the Miami hospital, they were kept from her side. They only received information on her condition when Lisa's sister arrived. Lisa died that night, without her family by her side. In the ensuing complaint by Lisa's family, Florida's federal court ruled that despite all the previous legal challenges, there was no duty or legal obligation to allow any visitors into a hospital. While they claimed this was the status quo, they were giving tacit permission for hospitals to continue to refuse certain visitors for any reason.

Only after the first of Karen Thompson's legal challenges did the public consciousness of Sharon Kowalski's case arise. It wasn't surprising for many in the Queer community, as one legal advocate made clear to the New York Times that, 'there is no other case that approaches this one in symbolic importance'. The case had 'touched the deepest nerve in the gay community across the United States because it triggers the two deepest fears of every gay person: a fight amongst loved ones and denial of personal wishes. In the beginning only local media reported on the case, but before long the national and international press caught on too. Concerts fundraising for legal fees were organised, Karen wrote a book, and she travelled the country gaining support and publicity from the Queer community and their allies. Sharon remained in the care home, hours away from her partner, believing Karen had left her. A national coalition of Queer groups rallied for the cause, there was even a National Free Sharon Kowalski Day, with celebrations and events in twenty-one cities across the United States. Vigils were held and marches stopped traffic to alert the world to the homophobic court system that refused to allow a Disabled woman to have visits from her partner. The lawyer who took on Karen's case said it 'became a real cause célèbre'. She spoke of how hard it was and how she struggled to get the courts and the reporters to accept that their relationship was valid and worthy of respect. One judge said in open court, 'you know it's a sin, don't you?' By the time late 1988 arrived, Sharon's father asked the court to appoint a new guardian, since he was too ill to continue in the role. Karen took the opportunity to file a petition to be named Sharon's new guardian. It was completely uncontested by anyone representing Sharon's parents or her wider family. Earlier that same year, medical staff had completed another mental capacity test and determined that far from the initial evidence, her mental age was that of a young child. She was more than able to express a clear preference for her ongoing care and life. This was in stark contrast to the suggestion and assumption that she was unable to understand questions put to her. In the run up to filing a petition for guardianship, Karen had been allowed some limited contact with Sharon. Sharon finally knew that Karen had never wanted to leave her. Despite the three witnesses opposed to Karen becoming the guardian, Sharon's preferences, along with the medical advice of many of her healthcare professionals were presented in court. All sixteen of the medical witnesses brought to court wholeheartedly supported Sharon's wish to return home with Karen and be cared for by her and her wife in the community. They spoke of how when Karen visited, Sharon was happier, relaxed, and more successful in her therapy, doing exercises they were never able to get her to do. They spoke of how she wanted to go home with Karen. However, the individual speaking out doesn't always help. Britney Spears is one of few specific examples who has fought their own guardianship order, as they are usually held behind closed doors and every US state's rules are different, to the extent that we don't know how many people in the United States are under guardianship orders.

In April 1991, 18 months after she submitted the only petition, the judge rejected Karen's request and appointed a friend of the Kowalskis, who happened to be one of the three opposing witnesses. She had never applied for the role, or even stated whether she would be capable of taking it on. While the judge recognised Karen's contributions, commitment, and knowledge, and noted Sharon's own preferences, the decision was made on three grounds. First, that Karen had allegedly made Sharon's sexual orientation public without her consent. Second, that she had established 'other domestic partnerships' (she had moved in with a new partner since Sharon's accident). Third, that Sharon's father would refuse to visit if Karen was her guardian. A well-known civil liberties leader said that this decision was considered by many to be 'a deep offense not only to all lesbians and gay men, but to all Americans who choose their partners and households by their own terms and not the legal rules imposed by society'. He believed, and most other people agreed, that 'Sharon chose her family. But the judge doesn't agree, so he imposed his own vision on her'. Even during Karen's petition and the subsequent hearing, evidence showed that the medical care being given by her father was substandard, and that Sharon's physical health had deteriorated under his guardianship. The nursing home he had selected for her primarily cared for elderly people, and the options for recreation and physical therapy had been minimal. On 17 December 1991, a court of appeal finally ruled in favour of Karen Thompson's petition, and by extension in favour of Sharon's wishes. Their attorney said, 'this seems to be the first guardianship case in the nation in which an appeals court recognised a homosexual partner's rights as tantamount to those of a spouse'. The court concluded that a trial court has wide discretion in guardianship proceedings, on this, the original court abused its discretion by denying Thompson's petition against the weight of the evidence in the case. It removed the family friend from Sharon Kowalski's guardianship and appointed Thompson in her place. The ruling said, 'all the medical testimony established that Sharon has the capacity to reliably express a preference in this case, and she has clearly chosen to return home with Thompson if possible. This choice is further supported by the fact that Thompson and Sharon are a family of affinity, which ought to be accorded respect'. This was believed to be the first legal confirmation in a US court that same sex partners could be considered a 'family of affinity', meaning they were treated equally to legal spouses. Previously this term had been used to refer to those who were adopted, couples of opposite sexes who were unmarried, and relations by marriage, such as in-laws or step-parents and children.

Soon after returning home, and under the care of Karen and her new wife, Sharon improved dramatically. For the first time in many years, she was standing for short periods of time and was able to speak well enough to put down her voice synthesizer and never used it again. Karen and her wife continued to campaign for the rights of disabled people as well as encouraging gay couples to think about advanced estate planning, so their wishes could never be ignored.

Due to the high-profile nature of this case, both the immediate and ongoing result for people across the country, whether they were gay or straight, was increased awareness of a Disabled person should be considered, even when it's assumed they don't have the capacity to express. This happened in the case of Patricia Peery when her brother filed for guardianship over her in 1996. While she was adamant that she didn't want her brother to be in control, nor see him, it was for courts to ask for limited evidence from a prospective guardian to convince them that guardianship was needed. Her case made it clear that determining incapacity and determining whether someone needed a guardian were two separate things.

Petitioning for guardianship means proving incapacitation, as well considering any additional support someone might have or any other outside influences. While the courts had determined

Patricia didn't need a guardian, her brother had appealed. He said that regardless of allowing her to live independently and make her own decisions, she was still incapacitated without support and she needed a guardian in the situation where her additional support wasn't present. The Supreme Court of Pennsylvania determined that these two separate issues needed consideration by the courts at the same time, and that, a person cannot be deemed incapacitated if his impairment is supported by friends or family or other support. They made it clear they would 'not disturb Ms. Peery's wishes as long as her decisions are rational and result in no perceivable harm to her'. The outcome of this case resulted in guardianship hearings changing their procedures in listening to the Disabled person themselves, and those who knew them best.

This became trickier when those wishes were expressed in the past. Determining the wishes of those who cannot express themselves, for example, patients in a persistent vegetative state, has long been, and continues to be, controversial. An unexpected cardiac arrest in 1990 catapulted Terri Schiavo into the public consciousness. After being resuscitated, she was left with severe brain damage and was the subject of a seven year long legal battle between her parents and her husband, fighting over whether the hospital should remove her feeding tube and allow her to die.

Since Terri hadn't left a living will, also known as an advanced directive, there was only one thing to do. A weeklong court trial was arranged to determine what Terri would have wanted, had she been able to communicate at the time. A total of eighteen different witnesses took the stand and gave evidence about Terri, her beliefs, and their opinions to allow the court to determine what she would have wanted. In this case the American Disability rights movement who were against assisted dying truly came together and used their experience from previous court cases to make the most impact. In the past they had allied with Democrats and 'left wing' groups, on this occasion they aligned with pro-life republicans.

The history of the Disability rights movement and their actions against assisted dying laws is a complicated one. The campaign group Not Dead Yet, has argued against laws that would allow for euthanasia for many decades. Many people fear these routes would be encouraged for disabled people, to remove the 'burden' of their care needs. This is not an unfounded fear, as recent reports from Canada, (who implemented Medical Assistance in Dying for non-terminal illness in 2021) show that some Disabled people have been pressured to apply for assisted death due to a lack of accessible housing and affordable healthcare. Throughout the 1980s several cases went to the courts where Disabled people wanted to be allowed to either refuse treatment and be released from their nursing homes into the community, or to remove life sustaining treatments and be allowed to die. This raised interesting implications and showed the priorities of the court system as they repeatedly determined that patients had a 'right to die', but not a right to live where they wanted to. ADAPT, (American Disabled for Attendant Programs Today as they were known then) began filing amicus briefs (an explainer written by experts on a specific topic to educate the courts), stating that having a choice between death and living in a nursing home was no real choice. While there was limited cross community response, these cases were well known amongst Disabled people's organisations, and were the subject of many articles and discussions. The Disabled people's movement was haphazard and disconnected. However, they united over Terri's cause and become more cohesive and were able to submit compelling evidence to the court to help win cases.

The first case with a unified response was of Robert Wendland in California. Both his wife and mother agreed that the medical diagnosis of his 'persistent vegetative state' was inaccurate, but his wife still wanted to remove his feeding tube. A state statute gave her the right to starve and dehydrate him, and forty-three different bioethicists wrote to the court to agree on that course of action. Ten separate disability groups aligned to argue against the presumption that no-one with his disabilities would want to live, and that he shouldn't have life-saving care removed based on that bias. The courts agreed with them. By 2003, a group of twenty-six distinct national disability rights groups had created the connections to be able to campaign together against court cases. Since then, the Disability rights movement has progressed from a disparate group of individuals with shared aims and little experience, to an international network of people and groups with shared goals, who can organise protests, arrange rallies, petition the courts, and pursue direct action to effect change. The idea of a broad 'disabled community' is a relatively new one. It was during the fight to implement Section 504 of the Rehabilitation Act in the US where a united disabled group, and 'Disabled people' as a recognised minority group, became accepted. The case of Sharon Kowalski was where the Queer liberation movement and Disability rights movement worked together for a common aim. While they were representing different parts of the issue, the networks they made allowed them to work together in the future, for people who were both gay and Disabled. At the time there was reluctance from Disabled campaigners to align with a gay rights campaign, and from Queer activists to interfere in a Disabled person's medical care.

It is also interesting to note how we learned about this story in the first place. The available sources that shed light on this, outside of the court documents, only speak from either the Queer angle or the Disabled angle, and very rarely both. Similarly, the entire story is only framed from the perspective of Karen Thompson, the non-disabled partner. This is understandable to many people, Sharon was kept in a home away from her community and was seen as unable to communicate for many years, and Karen was loud and visible. The framing of the issue in the public consciousness was primarily on the separation of a couple by a homophobic family, and never that a Disabled person had been needlessly institutionalised. Issues like this show why intersectionality within the communities is so important. For such a wide ranging and influential case to be reduced to these individual goals shows how we still don't understand our shared history.

Lord Byron

'Such a strange melange of good and evil'

When someone is so famous as to coin the term 'Byronmania', it's probably safe to say that they're not going to feature in any sort of list of unsung heroes. An early example of a celebrity and a 'regency superstar', the tales of his widespread affairs are well publicised and became so popular that women sent him locks of pubic hair. To many people this sounds outrageous and they believe it must be an urban myth. Was it even true? Well, yeah, pretty much.

Born in 1788 as George Gordon Noel Byron, the nineteenth

century bad boy and sex bomb (as Sir Tom Jones would say) inherited his lordship from his uncle aged 10, as his father (Mad Jack Byron) had long since died. However, the estate had accrued an impressive amount of debt, so while he was still privileged enough that he was a literal Lord, he had to go and look for the silver spoon to put in his own mouth when he was born. He was the sixth Baron Byron, born as the son of Mad Jack (also known as Captain John Byron) and his second wife Catherine. The aristocratic lineage of the Byron family goes back to Sir John Byron who was handed the whole of Newstead Abbey in Nottinghamshire as payment for his services to Henry VIII. With the family already in the service of the royals, by 1643, Charles I had appointed his descendent, yet another Sir John Byron, as a Baron.

He had been born with what was said to be a clubfoot, and as he grew older and became more active, wanting to play and run around, this began to cause him more and more physical and emotional pain. He hated that his foot looked twisted and grew more and more frustrated by how difficult it made doing what he wanted to do. His mother took him to a London surgeon in search of a cure, but she was unable to afford the treatment they suggested, as she was by now a single mother paying off the debts of her husband. As he got older, this impairment, and specifically the look of it, began to bother him more and more. This diagnosis of clubfoot is naturally contested since there is no way that anyone could make a diagnosis without an examination. Some think it was more likely to be a limb difference or 'birth defect' that wouldn't have been treatable, but others agree that the limb could have at least been improved with more prompt treatment. He remained very active, becoming a strong open water swimmer and participated in sport throughout his life. After they moved back to Scotland, where she had been raised by her grandmother, Byron's mother sent him to the local school to start his education, but he was deeply unimpressed by it. He said he learned very little there, and after just a year he left to be taught at home. He was primarily instructed by a local vicar who taught him to read, but also the son of the person who made his shoes, who taught him Latin. However, not long after this, Byron's mother suddenly learned that William, the fifth Lord Byron's grandson, had died at the battle of Calvi in Corsica on 31 July 1794, and that her son, who was six and a half at the time, was now the presumed successor to the Byron title and estates. Mrs Byron knew that this meant he would soon be in a position of influence and needed an education to back that up. His mother convinced the Treasury to grant Lord Byron a regular stipend for his education and living expenses, and they soon moved to a bigger city so that Byron could enter the Aberdeen Grammar School.

There he developed his passion for reading, although hilariously considering his future career, he said. 'I could never bear to read any Poetry whatever without disgust and reluctance'. He developed Scarlet Fever in either 1795 or 1796 (no-one seems to know for sure), and was sent to his Great-Grandmother's house in Banff, where Mrs Byron had grown up, to convalesce away from the city, since fresh country air was considered so important in the recovery from illnesses such as this. It was here that he was first able to truly appreciate the Scottish countryside and became enamoured with the scenery. This would be an obsession and an attachment that would forever stay with him and draw him back to Scotland.

He spoke extensively about his early romantic and sexual encounters in his later years. He was an early adopter of romance, saying later that he lost his virginity at a very early age. 'My first of flames' was his cousin Mary Duff. Years later, when reflecting on his love for her, Byron said, 'My love for her was so violent, that I sometimes doubt if I have been really attached since... [she] still lives in my imagination'. When the guy who had previously, up until this point, been known as Lord Byron died in May 1798, our Byron suddenly became the sixth Baron Byron of Rochdale at just ten years old. Suddenly, everything changed. A fancy lawyer, named John Hanson, known for his previous experience of helping the young and sudden heirs to estates and titles, had volunteered to represent Byron as he got used to the new life that his mother had little knowledge of. His first job was to arrange for Byron's legal guardian to be appointed. At this time, a child's father would have been the default guardian, but since Byron's father had died by this point, the guardianship didn't necessarily default to his mother. The lawyer's next task was to legally declare his client 'a ward in chancery'. This meant that he was placed under the protection of the Lord Chancellor. Mrs. Byron knew that they would have to uproot themselves and move to the estate that was now her young son's birthright. She sold their belongings and wrote to the chancellor to request an allowance to make sure Byron would have an appropriate standard of education and living. This would have been in the government's best interest, since Byron would be eligible to join the House of Lords and decide on laws and policy. A lot of people will have heard of the Houses of Parliament, but many may not know exactly what that means. In the UK, there are two different houses that make up Parliament, the House of Commons, and the House of Lords and both of them gather to work together in order to create the laws. The difference is that the House of Commons is made up of members who are elected by residents of a certain area to represent them, while the House of Lords is made up of those who have either inherited a title of Lord or who have been nominated. Thanks to several reforms in the House of Lords, there are now significantly fewer hereditary peers and most of the members of the House have instead been nominated for their work and achievements. At the end of August, mother and son (and an attendant for the young boy) left Scotland and headed for Newstead Abbey. The estate itself was massively in debt, and both the house and abbey had been so badly neglected that they were practically falling. The old Lord Byron hadn't been there much, and so had never bothered to maintain the property, and it was much the same story with a lot of other historic buildings in Rochdale that he also owned by birthright. Even so, when they arrived at the house, both Byron and his mother were awestruck by the history of the place, the story that it told and their heritage. It would take a lot of work, but they were certain that they could turn it into a home. With the allowance that she had managed to get from the government, Byron's mother was finally able to look for a doctor who could treat his clubfoot, although by leaving it so long to try and correct the position of his leg, the treatment was much more complicated, and significantly more painful. Through his desire to be cured of his 'deformity', he persevered and continued the treatments once he started to attend a boys' boarding school. There he was finally able to meet, befriend and spend time with boys who shared his newfound social status. He was said to have been bullied mercilessly for his leg brace by a whole range of people throughout his life, including his school chums. He was called a 'lame brat' amongst other charming names, and for most of the years of his schooling would continue having consistent treatments on his foot. He hated being seen as different or incapable, and he supposedly got so frustrated by having to wear a physical brace, that he threw it in the lake and carried on with all the same sports and physical activities that everyone else was doing. Many of his experiences during his later schooling at a series of fancy private schools, revolved around his intense 'friendships' with, often younger, fellow male pupils. Many sources state that 'it is not known that these were ever sexual' and so of course they determine that therefore any chance of a sexual relationship is completely implausible.

At seventeen and a half he went to Cambridge University, where he was incredibly unhappy. He said, 'I was miserable and untoward to a degree. I was wretched at leaving Harrow ... wretched at going to Cambridge instead of Oxford (there were no rooms vacant at Christchurch); wretched from some private domestic circumstances of different kinds, and consequently about as unsocial as a wolf taken from the troop'. However, he soon came to like Cambridge and both the luxurious lifestyle and casual approach to education it afforded, as well as the many good friends and 'very good friends' he made there, if you know what I mean. (And if you don't know what I mean, lovers). He ordered dozens of bottles of wine, sherry, and port to be delivered to his rooms. He never attended lectures, amassed a load of debt, developed a 'violent, though pure passion' for a young chorister and then after one term, he decided he didn't fancy university anymore and was instead going to go abroad for a few years, much to the alarm of his mother. Except he didn't really. He stayed in London, took fencing and boxing lessons, went to the theatre, and chased down a series of sexual encounters with sex workers and nobles alike, male and female.

Bisexuality is a difficult thing to determine in the past, as it wasn't a classification that a lot of people were very aware of, and so they likely wouldn't have identified themselves in that way. Similarly, as homosexual activity between men had been illegal for so long, it can be hard for researchers in the present to determine whether someone was bisexual, or they would have been homosexual if attitudes and laws allowed. And by hard, of course, I mean impossible. Most people however agree that Byron was bisexual. His passions for both women and men were not in any way a secret, either at the time or in the present day.

After a few months though he became bored of this and returned to Cambridge where he continued to run up huge debt and generally concern his mother. His pedantic resistance to the rules might have had something to do with it, after he objected to the college rules that he couldn't keep a dog, cat, or bird but they said nothing of other animals. Naturally, he figured that the obvious solution to this was to get a bear and keep it in his quarters. This may have contributed to Mrs Byron's view that he had a 'reckless disregard for money'. To escape her nagging, he spent his summer with friends, and used the time to put together a collection of his early poems. However, these aren't available as he almost immediately retracted all of the copies when he realised that some of the more 'warmly drawn' poems being dedicated to his cousin Mary would create a scandal. It didn't occur to him that others didn't have sexual feelings for their cousins.

He entered the House of Lords in 1809 because he had genuine ambition to work in politics, but he was seen by some as a supremely liberal rebel that the conservative factions needed to work together to get rid of. Part of this was down to his reaction to the Framework Bill, which would make destroying new mechanical looms, the cause of many fabric workers losing their jobs, punishable by death. Byron, quite reasonably, thought that was a bit extreme. He was often criticised by the rest of the political classes who compared his clubfoot to the Devil's cloven hoof. He wasn't keen on that, as he was very sensitive about his foot, to the extent that he didn't sleep in the same bed as his (extremely numerous) lovers. He was so sensitive about it that he went to a significant effort to hide that he had a foot at all, let alone a clubfoot. He would wear wide legged trousers, and even when he was so sick that he could barely move, just before he died, he still covered it with a sheet. He put so much effort into hiding his disability, that we're still not certain which leg it was. After reading an entire research paper debating which leg his clubfoot was on, I was no closer to an answer.

Like most young noblemen, he went on the Grand Tour after he left Cambridge which was essentially a gap year, but longer. Most would travel around Italy, France, Greece, learning about the classical arts, but Byron was different. He went to all the usual places, but he went much further east, visiting countries like Albania. He felt a real affinity with Albania, as shown by the famous painting of him kept in the National Portrait Gallery in Albanian traditional dress, which incidentally is one of a small number of portraits of him that exist from his own lifetime as he was so picky. Only a small number of paintings were sanctioned by him, and they had to flatter him. Many of the images we have of him were painted after he died, when artists didn't have to ask his permission anymore. Byron started his gap year in Portugal, where he also penned a letter to his friend Mr. Hodgson outlining what he had discovered about the Portuguese language: mostly swear words and insults. In these letters he revealed that the intention of his trip wasn't just to learn about culture and art and the world beyond his own shores, but to pursue more sexual experiences with men. Many of his travels were centred around these passionate and extremely numerous relationships, many with much younger boys and girls which, while obviously not acceptable, would have been much more common at the time. Many sources say that he was sexually abused as a child, and theorise that that may be why he viewed teenagers as viable potential sexual partners from when he himself was a teenager at boarding school.

It was the poetry he wrote on these travels that catapulted him to fame. After he returned, he gave a poem to his publisher which he didn't think very highly of, and to his surprise it was met with immediate and widespread critical acclaim. He said, 'I awoke one morning and found myself famous'. Biographers say, 'he quickly became the most brilliant star in the dazzling world of Regency London. He was sought after at every society venue, elected to several exclusive clubs, and frequented the most fashionable London drawing-rooms'. At first, he enjoys all the attention and welcomed his fame. His natural skill of self-promotion and his love of the limelight have led many people to call him 'the first rock star' and an early example of celebrity. It was his wife who coined the term 'Byromania' to describe the commotion that surrounded him. He very quickly became extremely well known and liked, highly sought after by all the brightest and best, but he was also famous for his promiscuity. He was famously described as, 'mad, bad and dangerous to know' by Lady Caroline Lamb, a married woman with whom Bryon had an incredibly widely known and well publicised affair. It was very obvious to everyone, and they were truly incapable of being subtle. Instead, when they were in public, they would insult each other and talk about how much they hated each other to throw their well-to-do pals off the scent. It didn't work. After a while he got bored and ended their relationship, quickly moving on to other society figures. In retaliation, she broke into his house dressed as a pageboy and in his office, grabbed a pen and scrawled 'remember me' across his notebooks, which arguably wouldn't have much of an effect unless she also signed her name. With his debts looming over him though, he began to consider that marriage might be a wise decision, despite a massive distaste for the whole idea. But before his search had even really got going, he got distracted by meeting his half-sister for the first time in many years. They spent a lot of time together and grew closer, and bonded over their shared father. Soon he forgot about his search for a wife. He has long been accused of having had an incestuous relationship with Augusta Leigh, but not in a way that anyone can ever prove, their time together just set society tongues wagging.

Despite having been so young when his father, Mad Jack died, Byron traced his 'horror of matrimony' to the 'domestic broils' of his parents and his famously rowdy father. Due to the sheer number of members of this family called 'Lord Byron' and 'Mrs Byron', I will for this next section be referring to 'our Byron' to mean the poet this chapter is about and 'Mad Jack' as his father. As it previously has, 'Mrs Byron' will refer to our Byron's mother and any other Byrons will be described individually as we go, because there are just so many of them. Mad Jack certainly had a reputation, and it wasn't as a good guy. He had been cut off by his father after half a lifetime of being wasteful, unreliable and being an unpleasant person. Mad Jack's father had eventually decided that enough was enough, and he couldn't let Mad Jack inherit all his money only to immediately spend the whole lot. After years of supporting him financially, he was finally sick of the nonsense and made the decision to both disown him and leave him to figure out life for himself. But Mad Jack, generally acknowledged as incredibly handsome, knew he could probably get by with his looks and his charm and get any woman he wanted, including one from a rich family. By 1778 he had given up on his normal job as a Coldstream Guard and decided that instead he was going to live the high life, join the stylish and influential circles and go to parties. In those circles he met Amelia D'Arcy, the marchioness of Carmarthen. They married in 1779 and soon had a daughter, Augusta Mary, who would be our Byron's half-sister and a major influence on his later life, although they didn't know each other well when they were young. A few years later though, Mad Jack was on his way to Bath on a quest for yet another wealthy wife. This was necessary for him after having lost his wife's £4000 a year income in January 1784, after her death. This was a major setback for him. He eventually decided on Catherine Gordon as a suitable replacement wife. Catherine's parents had both passed away when she was a baby, and her grandmother often known as Lady Gight, took her in and raised her at her home in Banff, Scotland. Most biographies describe her with frankly quite unnecessarily rude terms. They comment that Catherine, soon to be Mrs Byron, inherited a love of books and literature from her grandmother but say that despite being so widely read, she remained uneducated, sentimental, naive, chubby, and plain. She was just twenty years old when she met Mad Jack and it was said that she was swiftly won over by the dashing captain. On 13 May 1785, they were married at St. Michael's Church in Bath. Some of these biographies attribute her hasty decision to marry him to the idea that she was just so plain and boring and would never find a better suitor. By July, the newlyweds had relocated to Gight, close to Mrs Byron's childhood home in Banff, where Mad Jack quickly spent most of the £23,000 Catherine had contributed to their union from the money left by her parents (although much of it would have been immediately absorbed by Mad Jack's existing debts). After they moved to the Isle of Wight in July 1787, he ran away and travelled to Paris to avoid paying their (or rather, his) debts. The following September, Mrs. Byron joined him in Paris, by now pregnant with the baby who would be our Lord Byron, however just a few months later she got sick of him and all his mischief and left to return to London where she would soon give birth to her son. Mad Jack though, continued to be hounded by debt collectors and stayed constantly on the move with very little thought given to how or where his wife and son were. Even after Mrs Byron received a settlement to secure their home against the creditors, he was only ever present intermittently for the next two years, before moving to France with his sister in 1790 where he soon died of, we assume, consumption. He appointed his son 'Mr. George Gordon, heir of my real and personal estate, and charge[d] him to pay my debts, legacies, and funeral expenses' which was an interesting decision considering he wasn't even 4 years old, but I guess he wasn't expecting to die so soon. Despite how, I think it's safe to say, awful of a husband he'd been, Mrs Byron was devastated when he died.

Byron had seen how this affected his mother, and she was already concerned that he was going to turn out just like his father. Byron suspected that the apple didn't fall far from the tree and while he did eventually marry, it wasn't a happy relationship. He and his wife Anabella divorced after having one child, the famous computer engineer Ada Lovelace. Based on what we know of Byron, it seems reasonable to believe that her talent and achievements were despite Byron, rather than because of anything he did. The primary reason for the divorce was due to his philandering with all genders, however it was also clear that Anabella considered him legitimately insane. There had long been rumours of 'madness' running through the whole of the Byron family line, as may be clear from his father's nickname, and some of his behaviour only added to this assumption. However, what caused the most shock to his adoring public was that Byron's wife shared the suspicion that many researchers have had since then; that his half-sister's child might have been his. He also reportedly had numerous illegitimate children, but no-one was really surprised or even all that bothered about that. These rumours: his potential affair with his half-sister and his homosexual relationships, as well as his mounting debt, caused him to leave England in 1816 and never return. He wrote that in his last few weeks in England he was warned not to go out in public by his friends. He was ostracised and faced risks of violence from the public as well as many of his former friends.

It was after leaving England that he met and became friends with Mary Shelley and the members of her circle. He was with them at Lake Geneva, when the famous story of how Shelley's book Frankenstein came into being, was told. The short version is that it was a horrible, rainy and dark summer, due to a volcanic eruption in Indonesia which turned the skies dark. During this summer, the friends would tell each other ghost stories, and those stories became the basis of several excellent literary works, including, most famously, Frankenstein. He spent much of the next few years travelling around Europe, settling down for a while in Venice where he became friendly with the Armenian community that lived there, and fascinated by their language and culture, co-authoring several books on the Armenian language and the struggle for Armenian liberation. He is seen as an inspiration to many of the most historically renowned modern Armenian poets, which probably explains the portrait of him in traditional clothing from the country.

Around this time, Byron was writing the first parts of his most famous work; the satirical epic poem called Don Juan. The original story of Don Juan was a folktale of a Spanish libertine who dedicated his life to seducing as many women as possible, hence 'Don Juan' has since become a term to mean 'a womaniser'. In Byron's poem however, he twisted this whole idea on its head so that Don Juan wasn't a selfish man looking for pleasure and gratification at all costs, but an easily manipulated person who was repeatedly seduced by women who wanted to take advantage of him. The poem took place over 16 parts, but he never managed to finish it before he died. Several parts were published posthumously, but there wasn't any real attempt to finish the story, just to get it out and get the money for it. Initial critics said that the poem, and the story, was 'immoral' as it mocked many public figures and satirised many current events of his time, in such a way that there was no hiding who exactly he was talking about. And as everybody knows, a good-natured ribbing about what was going on in the world at the time is naturally 'immoral', and not 'a reasonable way to make a point without being aggressive'. While Byron later said that Don Juan was 'a work never intended to be serious', many people thought that it was 'a work of boundless genius'. However, all those people who had previously been okay with it, since it hadn't mocked them personally, suddenly changed their minds by the time the next few sections had come out in 1822, and upon reflection of the public's outrage, the publisher who had printed all his previous work, refused to carry on distributing it. Even so, it is the work he is most famous for, and is considered his magnum opus, as nobody loves a book more than the one they're not supposed to read.

He was vocally supportive of the Greek independence movement while he was living in Italy, and he was praised highly, particularly by the Greeks (obviously). He went there and paid the equivalent of thousands of pounds to restore all the Greek warships, telling them that he planned to continue and wanted to spend his entire fortune on the freedom of the Greeks. He was inexplicably given control of a rebel army, despite his lack of any kind of military experience, but before they had a chance to go anywhere, Byron contracted a fever and died. This moment is depicted in the famous painting, where his leg is covered by a sheet so that his clubfoot isn't visible, even as he's dying. It is said that he refused to show even the doctors who were treating him at the time. He is still a hero in Greece and is seen by many as the first example of a modern celebrity, with people (mainly women) sending him locks of hair (head and otherwise, as well as many, many other things…) but he said of himself, 'I am such a strange mélange of good and evil that it would be difficult to describe me'.

After Byron's death – in a bid to protect his reputation – his co-workers, associates and friends came together to burn his memoir, as well as any of his documents and papers that could reveal his homosexual desires to the public. Perhaps also to grieve his death, but this wasn't mentioned in any of the sources. As recently as 1950, a researcher was allegedly barred by Byron's publishing company from revealing details of his same-sex relationships. At the time Byron lived, the homosexual sex was still a crime punishable by death following the 1553 Buggery Act which was passed in the reign of Henry VIII. The actual law didn't state what they meant by 'buggery', but it was later determined by the courts to mean anal penetration and bestiality, but not oral penetration.

Years after his death, a new poem surfaced. The title page of the book that published Don Leon stated that it was 'Part of the Private Journal of His Lordship, Supposed to Have Been Entirely Destroyed'. It is now widely assumed that it wasn't written by Byron as it contains references to a lot of things that happened in the 1830s that he couldn't have known about, since he was dead. However, it seems to contain a lot of personal details about his relationships at university and while travelling, as well as intimate knowledge of his life and the workings of the House of Commons while he was there as a peer. Only someone very close to him would have known all of this, although it wasn't thought to be widely known that Byron had same sex relationships, so researchers can only assume that it wasn't published by someone who cared about his ongoing reputation. It may well have had multiple authors, which makes sense since the poem stretched to fifty pages. However, having read it, it's clear that it was a celebration of homosexual love, a call for the removal of the death penalty for buggery and sodomy, and a plea for tolerance for men who loved men. It argued that homosexuality was a normal part of life, and there was no need for it to be against the law.

Buggery is the English term which means the same as sodomy, a term used to cover both anal sex and bestiality, although it's worth noting that sometimes sodomy can also refer to any 'non-procreative sexual activity'. It remained a crime punishable by death until 1861, although no executions had been carried out since 1836 when James Pratt and John Smith were hanged after being found together in a private room. It wasn't until 1861 that the new Offences Against the Persons Act was passed, and the death penalty for buggery was removed. Instead, the sentence was ten years in prison, which was obviously much better. However in 1885, they made it much worse again when The Criminal Law Amendment Act extended this from just buggery to making any homosexual act illegal. In many court cases, all that was needed was a letter between two men expressing affection. The capacity of this law to be used for evil was so well known that it was often referred to as 'The Blackmailer's Charter' and many people fell for it, including Oscar Wilde. The laws didn't include sexual relationships between women, but in contrast to the myth that Queen Victoria couldn't believe that women would do such a thing, the reality was likely to be a bit more boring and was just because women had never been mentioned in the laws before, and so it would be weird to suddenly bring them up. Lesbianism was believed to have affected such a small number of women that it was thought by some people that even bringing the idea to public attention would encourage women to go out and have sex with women, much like how people seem to think that giving teenagers sex education will give them the idea to go out and have sex, when they'd otherwise never have considered the notion. Not much changed until after the Second World War, when the sheer number of men with distinguished service careers who were being prosecuted, started to make people question the harshness of the punishments for these consensual sexual acts which were conducted in private. The best example of this is the sad case of Alan Turing, the world-renowned code breaker.

The first reference to the 'Byron' poem Don Leon seems to have been in 1853, when someone wrote a letter to the journal *Notes and Queries*, saying that they had read it abroad. It was 1863 when it was first published in Britain by a man who allegedly sold mainly pornography and genuinely believed it was by Lord Byron, to the point that he supposedly tried to blackmail the family with it. History does not record how that attempt went but given there is no record, I'm going to take a stab in the dark at 'poorly'. It caused a great stir, whether it was by the famous poet, or he was using his name to effect the desired publicity. For something to so openly campaign for homosexual men to not just be left alone, but embraced by society as normal, was something so far out of the norm that it caused outrage for many decades. In 1934, a publisher tried to print the poem again, all the copies were confiscated and destroyed by the police on the grounds that it was obscenity.

As we now know, this poem didn't prompt any kind of major change, but it's fair to say it probably loosened the minds of a lot of people towards the idea that homosexual relationships happened. While nothing as simple as a poem could make them accept it as normal and natural, inevitably becoming familiar with the idea it would make it easier for the next couple. Even though Lord Byron wasn't the one who wrote this (probably), it's clear that it was a subject he would have agreed with, even if he wouldn't have risked his reputation for it in his lifetime. His rumoured homosexual relationships led him to flee the country of his birth, but the idea that Britain's favourite poet might have been gay would mean that other people wouldn't have to hide from society in future.

Alan Turing

'A rather painful interest for a young man'

For many decades, no-one was allowed to know why Alan Turing was so famous, and until 2013 he was a criminal in the eyes of the law. Now of course he's not only recognised as a national hero and the victim of a significant miscarriage of justice, he's also the face of the fifty-pound note! What greater honour could there be? Other than the pride of knowing that the lives of around fourteen million people are thought to have been saved by your work, and the entirety of the Second World War was shortened by an estimated two years. This soon to be prodigal son of Julius Mathison and Ethel Sara Turing was born on 23 June 1912. Alan Mathison Turing was the youngest child of a father who worked in the Indian Civil Service, and a mother who was the daughter of the chief engineer of the Madras railway. While they were living and working in India, Alan and his brother were sent to live in foster homes in England (in this case an arrangement for relatively posh children with parents living abroad rather than the modern-day usage) and attended private preparatory schools that would be considered appropriate for two young boys of their class. By no means were they the landed gentry, but they were upper middle class, and the family had an aspiration for a higher status. Alan was always interested in science, to an extent that was deeply concerning for his mother. His hobby was creating experiments outside of his school hours, as he was most interested in finding a way to use 'the thing that is commonest in nature and with the least waste of energy'. But at this time, private schools for well off boys were primarily focused on the arts and humanities subjects, languages, history, and philosophy. The headmaster told his mother that 'if he is to be solely a scientific specialist, he is wasting his time at a Public School'. Although Turing's private notes on the theory of relativity demonstrated a degree-level understanding, he was almost blocked from earning his school certificate in case he brought the reputation of the institution into question by not being good at Latin. He wasn't particularly interested in the 'classics' subjects, but played along as much as he needed to. Christopher Morcom, a very talented fellow student in the year above him at the Sherborne school, was the only person who provided the motivation for discussion and challenge. They formed a fast and close relationship, partly due to the intellectual stimulation that neither had experienced before and partly because Turing was deeply infatuated with him. It's difficult to say whether Christopher felt the same or just saw Alan as a platonic best friend. Unfortunately, he died suddenly in 1930 and so we'll never know. That loss of friendship and companionship led to a long period of grief, and Turing's response to that was to commit a great deal of time and effort to doing what Morcom was now unable to achieve. He began to wonder if the human consciousness could be liberated from matter by dying, and how the human mind was embodied in matter. He also wrote several letters to Morcom's mother in which he theorised on the nature of life and death which may not have been appreciated by a woman grieving her son.

He was admitted to King's College in Cambridge to study mathematics and became more comfortable within himself there. There were many openly gay people studying at King's College. Unlike many of his homosexual brethren he wasn't particularly interested in literature or the arts, and while they spent their time discussing their reading lists, he was much more at home with sport and sailing. Almost immediately after graduating in 1934, he was given a fellowship by his old college in recognition of his exceptional work on probability theory. He was on his way to a career as an academic researcher and lecturer until he decided that he wanted a new challenge. In a letter supporting his fellowship, one of his instructors said that Turing had a 'rather painful interest' in calculable numbers. Even though this mathematician's path for his life was before him, he decided to ignore it and go in a completely different direction. He became interested in mathematical logic, and in a specific problem called the *Entscheidungsproblem*. The

'Decision Problem', as it's also called, is an important concept in both maths and computer science which asks if there is a set of rules (an 'algorithm') that will reliably tell you whether a mathematical statement is true or false. Originally, the way they determined whether methods of working out the validity of a statement were effective, was based on whether a human could replicate it. Turing, however, invented a machine that would test these – an early computer. From all this work, from the months and months of building, studying, theorising, and testing he finally had an answer to the decision problem. And that answer was 'no'. No, there was no possible reliable algorithm that could prove every mathematical problem. Meaning that our systems of counting are not provable. Arguably, there is no such thing as maths. Another mathematician, A. Church, an American with a higher profile, happened to arrive at the same conclusion at the same time, using a different method, and so Turing's academic paper was delayed. He was invited to Princeton University in America to advance his theory and managed very successfully. Not only did he prove his Turing machine could compute everything a human could but also proved his theory was as relevant as Church's, and in fact better. His Turing machine advanced computer science by showing the principles of programming. While he was in the United States, the atmosphere in Europe was growing tense. The prospect of another war was becoming likely, and with the advances in technology that had occurred since the First World War, would affect a very different conflict. He decided to take a break from his academic career and make an electromagnetic cipher machine. In what may have been a very strange decision, he left America to return to Cambridge. He attended lectures outside of his field and argued with professors about the nature of maths, far from the world-renowned work he was doing at Princeton. It was deeply confusing for the lecturers and other students to have a renowned researcher come back and hang out with undergrads. Secretly he was working with the Government Code and Cypher School. This unit of the UK government was attempting to decipher a series of secret codes being used by Germany to send intelligence and plan military action. One of those was Enigma.

It's easy when wars have a definite beginning and end date, to forget that there's usually a long period of time before it starts. The army moved around while strategy was being made, and for a large group of people there is no dramatic difference in their jobs once war is officially declared. It may add a sense of urgency, but this is what they were planning for the whole time. By the time Alan Turing and his co-workers arrived at Bletchley Park after the declaration of war, they'd already been trying to crack Enigma for a while. The level of secrecy they were forced to agree to, was such that most never spoke of it for the rest of their lives and would have prepared lies when asked about their roles during the war. Researchers have since said, 'there was a special ceremony where the importance of secrecy was drummed into their heads' with the threat of severe criminal consequences if they didn't comply and even when the war ended, 'the head of Bletchley Park sent a memo reminding everyone that the code of silence applied not just during wartime but forever'. It was only in 1974 that people began to learn of what happened in Bletchley when one of the codebreakers finally got the permission of the government to publish a book about the war. Many family members of those mentioned were amazed to learn of the impact that their relatives had had on the history of the world. The level of secrecy was so strict that two research papers that Turing wrote while working there were decided to be so sensitive that they were restricted by the National Archives until 2012, meaning that no-one, not even researchers, were allowed to see them. At Bletchley, they started with 200 staff members, mostly taken from the upper reaches of Oxford and Cambridge, but they realised they needed more bodies and brains – and a wider variety of people in order to collect the expertise they needed – that soon expanded to students, civil servants and anyone who had a knack for puzzles. By the end of the war the staff totalled 9,000, three quarters of whom were women.

The Polish codebreakers were the real success story though. They had been working on Enigma for much of the 1930s and had found a way to penetrate those messages. It was the help of the Poles that allowed Bletchley to receive the messages they needed to decode. Building on an existing machine, Turing and his team managed to create a general version that decoded secret messages even when the primary key had been changed. By the end of 1939, his machine was working and had decoded several messages, but it wasn't until eighteen months later when it could be used to reliably crack the codes. It required much more data from the Navy and very complicated statistics to allow it to be used regularly. While Enigma may be the most famous code to have been broken in Bletchley, it's far from the only one, and their work was nowhere near over. For many years, employees were decoding messages from all levels of the war effort. Some were messages about food rations and soldiers' leave, others allowed them to read enemy flight signals and know where the Luftwaffe would be flying.

Turing was an unusual figure, rather than being ostracised and mocked as before, he was seen as an eccentric genius by his colleagues. Known as 'Prof', others at Bletchley said he had terrible hayfever and would 'cycle to the office wearing a service gas mask', would chain his favourite mug to the radiator so it didn't get lost and would frequently run the forty miles to London meetings (often arriving before those who had taken public transport). When his bike chain started coming off, instead of getting it fixed he counted how many cycles of the pedals he'd done, then jumped off to adjust it by hand. He also 'had a habit of saying ah-ah-ah-ah-ah... which made it difficult to interrupt his line of thought or have a line of thought of one's own!' He had difficulties with the other kids at school and didn't have many friends or acquaintances due to a 'social impairment'. He had such poor handwriting that an examiner said he lost marks frequently – because his work was illegible, and sometimes because 'misreading his own writing led to mistakes'. He did not look anyone in the eye and struggled with both social norms and literalness, leading most people to believe now that he was Autistic. A research paper from 2003 concluded that he had Asperger's Syndrome, although more recently it is believed that Asperger's, a development disorder, isn't a separate diagnosis and is just another word for being on the autistic spectrum. Historically, Asperger's was used as a term for those who didn't have an additional learning disability, and instead were 'high functioning', another term which is no longer used by Autistic campaigners and scholars as functional abilities change frequently depending on what an activity is, what adjustments have been and a million and one other factors.

Unusually, for a gay man, he proposed to one of his female colleagues. This co-worker was admired by him for her critical thinking and her abilities at her job, and got on well with him. Even though she accepted, he had second thoughts almost immediately. He eventually confessed and revealed his homosexuality, but she was completely nonplussed and didn't see that as a reason to call off their engagement. He decided that he couldn't go through with it and broke it off. They remained on good terms and continued working together.

In 1942 he was shipped to America to try to find a technological solution for encrypting conversations between Winston Churchill and Franklin D. Roosevelt. This took many months, and he was gone for so long that in his absence the German Navy changed their Enigma codes again. While his voice secrecy machine project ran in the background, once he returned to England he began his next big project, the electronic Turing machine. With this, he would be able to automate the codebreaking for the war effort but use a similar machine to read any algorithms and programmes. He was inventing the digital computer. This is the first design of an electronic computer as we understand it today, but once again some Americans stole his thunder by releasing a paper on it first. This development prompted the National Physical Laboratory in London to act and start building computerised machines. They recruited Turing after the end of the war to build a computer of their own, and he delivered. He built the plans for the Automatic Computing Engine (ACE), which could decipher codes, do complex maths, or play chess. It was said to be 'the first complete specification of an electronic stored-program all-purpose digital computer'. However, his colleagues thought it was too complicated, not to mention they were slightly sceptical it would work at all, given that Turing was legally prohibited from explaining some of the proof of its viability, because it occurred during his work at Bletchley. So, they built a smaller version with less memory and fewer capabilities, which was overshadowed before it was finished by a better 1948 creation from the Royal Society Computing Machine Laboratory in Manchester. His earlier concepts had been a major part of the design of the Mancunian computer, and so he took up an essentially ceremonial role there soon after. During this period, he wrote the first ever programming manual, and began developing his theories on AI, or artificial intelligence. In what could be seen as an echo of the present day, he was fascinated by how closely this computer would be able to acquire human brain functions and whether it would be able to develop artificial intelligence. There's a very good reason that the Turing test is named after him. The Turing test, also known as the imitation game, tests if artificial intelligence can behave indistinguishably from a human. In the test, a human assessor would have two typed text-based conversations, one with a computer and one with a human, and if the human assessor was unable to tell which was a human and which was a machine, the machine passed the test.

Turing had never hidden his homosexuality. He had relationships with men while at Cambridge and though he knew it was against the law, he never saw anything wrong with it. He was arrested after he called the police for help. His house had been burgled and while they were investigating, Turing was able to tell them the name of the person who broke in. When they found out that the criminal and the victim had met through a connection with another man, Arnold Murray, they asked about Turing's relationship with Arnold. Turing told them the truth, that they were lovers and the police promptly forgot about the burglary and arrested both Alan Turing and Arnold, eventually charging them with 'gross indecency'. This was a charge which criminalised lower-level sexual activity between men that couldn't be legally considered sodomy (or 'buggery') as there was no proof of penetration. Turing didn't even attempt to deny it or defend himself in court, because he didn't think he'd done anything that required him to defend himself. He was given two choices by the judge. Prison or two years on oestrogen hormone therapy.

Far from being socially outcast while at Bletchley, several colleagues spoke as character witnesses in his defence. 'Their testimony explained – without giving away any secrets – how significant Alan's wartime contribution had been.' Some believe that he was targeted as a relatively high-profile individual, since while most cases of this nature would have had one charge, the police had put a total of six charges on them. The hormone therapy he was given was a form of chemical castration that reduced the sexual urge; even though it would do nothing to stop them being gay, it would stop them wanting to have sex until the treatment was discontinued. While this was a barbaric thing to force someone to do, it was said to be a softening of attitudes for the British establishment by considering homosexuality as a disease that needed to be treated medically, rather than a moral failing and perversion that needed to be punished. Considering the side effects, he was said to have possessed an 'amused fortitude', writing that 'no doubt I shall emerge from it all a different man, but quite who I've not found out'. He continued to be consulted by the British secret services long after the war due to his knowledge and expertise, but once he was convicted, he lost his security clearance and was no longer able to work with GCHQ on Cold War related, or any other, projects. This was a blow to him and left him with free time. He soon became fascinated by biology and the natural sciences, setting up laboratories in his home in which he experimented.

In 1954, two years after his hormone treatment ended, he was found dead in his home by his housekeeper. Beside him was a half-eaten apple. Based on an inquest that was performed on the same day, it was determined he had committed suicide via cyanide poisoning, although the apple was never tested and there was very little investigation into the circumstances of his death. His mother believed that he had accidentally ingested cyanide from the fumes of his experiments, and there was no evidence provided that his mental state was disturbed. Some have theorised there could have been state involvement in his death but it sounds a bit farfetched. He was privately cremated in Woking. As time passed, more secrets were revealed about the work at Bletchley and how much it had impacted the outcome of the war, but it was only in the early 2000s when the public started becoming more aware of what had happened to Alan Turing after the war. It wasn't until 2009 that Turing really returned to prominence, in the form of a public petition calling for an official apology to both him and his descendants for his appalling treatment. This petition had been started by a fellow computer scientist, John Graham-Cumming, via the then relatively new UK government ePetitions website. It called for the government to 'recognise the tragic consequences of prejudice that ended this man's life and career'. As we've already seen, the reason for his untimely death is debated and unknowable, but for many people, the loss of the workplace where he thrived and the years of chemical castration were enough to warrant an official apology. But this was far from the standard kind of online petition, started and then forgotten about while you browse some other parts of the internet. John campaigned for this cause, contacting the press, appearing on television and weeding out the famous names who had signed it to get them to expand its reach. Soon he had 30,000 signatures, far above the 500 required to get a response from the government, but he wasn't going to stop there. Turing's surviving relatives got in touch with their support for the campaign and with their approval it wasn't long before the government at the time took notice. Graham-Cumming was in bed with the flu when he spoke to Gordon Brown, UK Prime Minister, who read the text of the apology that he would release just thirty minutes later. In it, he wrote that 'the debt of gratitude he is owed makes it more horrifying…that he was treated so inhumanely' by the government, admitting that he 'deserved so much better'. Despite this apology, many people thought this wasn't enough. He was still legally a criminal. But there was a change of government, and everything was forgotten about.

In 2012, the UK's National Archives were finally allowed to start showing people some of Alan Turing's wartime documents. These showed just how much he had contributed to our intelligence service's knowledge of codebreaking and the country's security. It reinvigorated people to the idea that Turing didn't deserve to have a criminal record for something that was no longer illegal. A series of private member's bills in both the House of Commons and the House of Lords were all put forward in 2012 to raise awareness and public support for an official overturning of his conviction. But before any of these could get through the houses, Chris Grayling, the Justice Minister at the time, sent a request to the Queen that Turing should receive a royal pardon, as the government had recognised the unfair and discriminatory treatment he endured because of the legislation in effect at the time. This pardon was granted under the Royal Prerogative of Mercy, intended for people convicted of crimes in England and Wales. This was generally used for situations where the person was innocent of the crime and a family member had requested it, and although neither of these criteria were met, he was still granted this pardon in recognition of his achievements and how unjustly the government had treated him. The government said that 'a pardon from the Queen is a fitting tribute to an exceptional man'.

But there were thousands of other men who had been convicted under these same laws. This Royal Pardon led to a campaign to overturn the convictions of everyone who had been taken to court and convicted of being gay. There were numerous attempts to put forward an Alan Turing Law; this would grant a pardon to everyone who was convicted of acts that were no longer offences, but due to various procedural reasons were never effected. Turing's Law, as it is known informally, was eventually introduced as an amendment to the Police and Crime Act that would grant a posthumous or an automatic pardon, for those still alive. It was given Royal Assent on 31 January 2017 and the pardon was implemented immediately. While there was frustration from some quarters that this wouldn't pardon people who were convicted of acts that were technically still offences, but not routinely charged, and the acknowledgement that those laws had been wrong, and not just different or 'a product of a different time', was a major step forward.

Turing hadn't been the only one though. There had been a massive increase in prosecutions of homosexual men in the 1950s, and people were starting to think these punishments weren't proportionate. Several high-profile men, many of whom had served their country admirably during the war and had rightfully been considered heroes, had been prosecuted and the public shaming of being hauled into court was almost worse than any sentence the court could give. Many thought that in private, who cared what they did if it wasn't hurting anyone? Sensing the beginning of this sea change, the government set up a committee to investigate whether the existing legislation needed to be changed. It spent 3 years considering the issue, particularly the scientific evidence that homosexuality was not a disease or a mental illness that could be, or needed to be, cured. John Wolfenden was appointed as chair to the Departmental Committee on Homosexual Offences and Prostitution by the Home Secretary, Sir David Fyfe, who strangely later strongly opposed any advancement of gay rights. Part of the theory goes that by sending the issue to a committee, Fyfe was hoping to kick the whole idea into the long grass so they wouldn't have to deal with it. Unfortunately for him, Wolfenden, an experienced teacher and well-respected authority on education and social issues, took this role seriously and in 1957 they published the Wolfenden Report. This report recommended the decriminalisation of all homosexual acts between consenting adults above the age of 21. And they were blistering in their justification for such a drastic move. 'Unless a deliberate attempt be made by society through the agency of the law to equate the sphere of crime with that of sin, there must remain a realm of private activity that is in brief, not the law's businesses. In short: mind your own business, just because you don't agree doesn't mean it should be against the law. Potentially predicting a backlash, Harold Macmillan and his government decided they weren't going to do anything about this report or its recommendations, and they would pretend it didn't exist. In fact, the House of Commons voted down a motion that would have shown support for the recommendations of the report by a majority of 114. However, five years later another vote on decriminalising private gay relationships for over 21-year-olds prompted by the MP Leo Abse still failed, but by only nineteen votes.

By later that year, in October 1965, many people in both Houses of Parliament were in support of relaxing the laws on homosexuality. The House of Lords supported the recommendations of the Wolfenden Report, and in 1966 when the Sexual Offences Bill came through Parliament, Leo Abse MP saw an opportunity to propose a new bill, almost entirely identical but with one addition, to decriminalise some homosexual relationships. The government, by now a Labour government run by Harold Wilson, realised this had broad support, and so allowed the incredibly cheeky move. This came during the period known as 'the permissive society', where the government legalised abortion, relaxed divorce laws, and abolished the death penalty, it was a popular time for social change. It's worth noting the leadership itself didn't care about creating laws for moral issues, but the Labour Party MPs and membership did, and to the majority it seemed sensible to listen to them. The Sexual Offences (No.2) Bill passed both the Houses of Commons and Lords and received Royal Ascent on 27 July 1967. The bill legalised sex between men, if it was in private, the two men were over twenty-one, they were in England or Wales, and they weren't in the Army, Navy or Air Force. So, while there were still a lot of conditions for these relationships, the punishments for those acts not covered by the law were reduced and dependent on which of the requirements they had broken. However, the law didn't change attitudes overnight. Gay men were given a warning when the bill was passed, with one Lord saying that 'any form of ostentatious behaviour now or in the future or any form of public flaunting would be utterly distasteful ... [And] make the sponsors of this bill regret that they had done what they had done'. It wasn't until 1980 that Scotland introduced laws which matched those in England and Wales and 1982 for Northern Ireland.

While many people consider this as the point at which homosexuality was decriminalised in England and Wales, there was still a disparity in the age of consent, as well as the very strict terms of 'private'. Until 2003, it was illegal for a third person to be present, even consensually, while two men were having sex. In 1994 the age of consent for gay men was reduced to 18, and finally in 2000 it was reduced to 16, the same as for heterosexual sex. The offences of gross indecency and buggery were eventually repealed altogether in 2003, finally removing the crime of gay people existing and wanting to have sex. In 2020, a Freedom of Information request revealed that the Royal

Mint had considered creating a commemorative coin to mark the 50th anniversary of the decriminalisation of homosexuality. They eventually decided against it because they didn't think the type of people who collect commemorative coins would be interested in collecting a coin related to gay rights. While everyone loves a £50 note with Alan Turing's likeness, perhaps a 50p piece for all the gay men in England and Wales was a step too far.

Barbara Jordan

'As cozy as a piledriver'

After the Watergate Scandal became known to the public, it sent shockwaves across America, a development that hardly surprised anyone. It was only the second time in history that the American Congress had ever been asked to consider a president's impeachment, and the first time it was televised. Everyone, from the government to the public, was quite surprised that Barbara Jordan, a member of Congress in her first term, had been included on the investigating committee. As the newest member of Congress, and therefore the lowest in the pecking order, her opening remarks were delivered at the end of the day to allow the more senior members to speak. As the evening broadcast reached its prime time slot for television viewers, Barbara Jordan took to the podium to deliver a pivotal speech. With her words, she implored the committee, and all American people, to take the constitution seriously, it seemed like the whole country had stopped to listen.

Barbara hadn't always been as confident. When Barbara first started school, she preferred to talk to her friends than listen to her teachers and learn. However, her very strict parents soon changed her and instilled a sense of discipline and responsibility. She had been an intelligent child, but to avoid the scolding and spankings, she dedicated herself to becoming the best student. The importance of education was impressed upon the whole family from a young age, with Barbara later remembering that her mother, father, and sisters all said, 'You're never going to amount to anything unless you go to school. You've got to get something in your head.' According to her family, this was more important for her than it was for her sisters. They placed a particularly high value on her education. Her father was distressed when she was born in 1936, supposedly saying to her mother, 'why is she so dark?' His concern wasn't baseless, it was much harder to be dark skinned in Houston, Texas, as the city's racist dynamics often favoured lighter-skinned African Americans. Her family knew that she would have to work much harder in the segregated Deep South to achieve the same success as her fairer friends, and so her parents pushed her to excel academically. As the youngest daughter of a Baptist minister and a teacher, Barbara Jordan was a naturally talented speaker and orator. She didn't realise it at first, but once she discovered that she could make people listen to the power of her words by speaking, she began to realise her true potential. Encouraged by a high school teacher, she joined her first debate team and found herself drawn to public speaking. At Phillis Wheatley High School, a segregated institution for African American students, Jordan excelled academically and at extracurricular activities, earning both Girl of the Year and the President of the Honor Society. Her school was for Black students only and named after Phyllis Wheatley, the first published African American poet, who was educated by her masters due to her chronic asthma and literary talent. After her book was published, she was freed from slavery, an inspiring example of the power of education and creativity. All of Barbara's energies were dedicated to hard work, to becoming the best student, so that she could achieve anything she wanted to in her life. She devoted her uncertain teenage years to her studies. But it was a chance encounter at school in her 10th grade year that changed everything. A remarkable guest speaker, Edith Spurlock Sampson visited their class. Edith Spurlock Sampson was an African American lawyer, and had made history by working with the National Association for the Advancement of Coloured People (NAACP), the League of Women Voters, and the National Council of Negro Women. She was the first Black delegate for the United States appointed to the United Nations, and the first Black woman to be elected as a judge in Illinois. She is probably best known for stating that while there was no racial equality in the US, 'I would rather be a Negro in America than a citizen in any other land'. The speech Sampson delivered to the rapt school children made Jordan feel like the most important thing she could do with her life was to become a lawyer. As Jordon reflected on why she made the decision to pursue a career path that was so hard and would involve so much work and adversity, she said that 'I can stay comfortable or go out in the world.' Inspired by her new-found direction in life and her love of public speaking, she entered the Oratorical Usher's Contest, winning the National Championship and a $200 scholarship to any university in the country.

However, for Jordan, this prize presented a bitter reality, because due to Texas' segregation policies, she couldn't go to any college. The University of Texas made some concessions by allowing some Black students, but only for graduate study, and only for programmes that weren't covered by the African American universities of Texas Southern and Prairie View. However, it would take two more years for the University of Texas to break its colour barrier and admit their first Black undergraduate student. Until then, the prevailing attitude was that Black students were already receiving an education at their designated universities, so why should they be admitted to their predominantly white Universities? Jordan went to Texas Southern University, a traditionally Black college in Houston. Given her level of success while in high school, she joined the debating society at college, further developing her natural skill in public speaking that had allowed her to thrive at school and further develop her confidence and authority as a speaker. This debate team achieved more than anyone expected, competing with impressive Ivy League universities, beating students from Yale and Brown Universities and drawing with many others including Harvard, which was long regarded as the country's best debating team. Many people were surprised they had managed so well against Harvard, as it was assumed that historically Black universities were going to be ineffectual against the Ivy League teams. If they could compete with Harvard, they could compete with anyone.

After graduating from university, Jordan's passion for law remained steadfast. She took the next stage of her plan and was accepted into the programme at the prestigious Boston School of Law. However, she soon discovered how much more difficult the academic rigour of law school demanded. She had to work much harder to maintain the same level of success, and the pressure took a toll on her well-being. Jordan remained committed to being the best student she could be, and just skating through for a solid pass was never going to be acceptable, she wanted to be the best. She later said that 'I didn't get much sleep those years. I was lucky if I got three - four hours a night ... I had to stay up. I had to'. Finishing her degree with anything less than distinction was not an option. Instead, she graduated from law school as one of only two African American women to graduate, who both happened to be from Houston, Texas. The next step was the Bar exams, a notoriously arduous series of exams which you needed to pass to practise law. Jordan excelled, passing with flying colours. After a year of teaching at the Tuskegee Institute in Alabama, she returned to Texas to set up her own law practice from her parents' kitchen table.

As a student of political science and history, Barbara had always been interested in and knowledgeable about politics. However, it wasn't until the 1960 presidential election that she became a volunteer, dropping leaflets and knocking on doors to try and get Democrat John F. Kennedy, and his running mate, Lyndon B. Johnson (the Texan senator), elected. At one of the campaign events in a Black church, a representative from the campaign didn't show up due to a last-minute illness and so, with zero notice at all, Barbara delivered an impassioned speech, imploring the crowd to vote Democrat at a time when many African Americans were switching to the Republicans. 'I was startled with the impact I had on people,' she said. 'Those people were just as turned on and excited as if some of the head candidates had been there to talk about the issues.' This serendipitous opportunity brought her to prominence in the local chapter of the Democrat party. She became a regular fixture at rallies and her friends thought she would be the perfect person to represent her community in government. Such was their faith in her that one of her friends donated the $500 registration fee that she needed to run for the Texas House of Representatives in 1962. For those unfamiliar with the difference in the American political houses, the House of Representatives is the lower House of Congress, with the Senate being the higher. While both are technically Congress, the members of the House of Representatives are usually referred to as 'Congressman' and 'Congresswoman' while those from the Senate are called 'Senator'. Despite being a first-time candidate, Jordan knew that even if every Black resident voted for her, it wouldn't be enough to secure a victory. In that race, as expected, she was unsuccessful, but she remained undeterred and was determined to run again. Most of Jordan's legal practice largely comprised of wills and divorces of people who were referred from her parents' church. However, she remained determined to shift the direction of her career into politics. She was incredibly popular among the Texas Democrats, both for her remarkable public speaking skills and breath of fresh air that emanated from having a well-educated and eloquent Black woman as a visible part of their party. Of course, this has a shallow ring of tokenism to it, and realistically many of the local Democrats saw her as an opportunity to try and win back the African American vote from the Republicans, but Barbara didn't care, as long as voters supported her campaigns. She ran again in 1964, but again was unsuccessful. Her advisors came to her, presenting a theory about why she was losing. Jordan's reputation among Texas Democrats was built on her public speaking skills, her tertiary education and articulation, however, she had been accompanied on the campaign trail by a close female 'companion', and some of her advisors worried about her future chances at winning an election if people knew she 'preferred the company of women'. Jordan knew there was nothing the matter with being a lesbian, but she would have to be more discreet to achieve her goals. After meeting Nancy Earl, the educational psychologist who would become her long-time partner and occasional speechwriter, she would thinly veil their relationship as a close friendship.

Jordan's concerns were not unfounded. In 1953, President Eisenhower had signed an executive order banning 'people with a sexual perversion' or gay people like her from working in federal jobs. The order remained in place for twenty years, and while members of Congress are not technically federal employees, Barbara would have been aware of the sentiment toward gay staff within government. However we consider LGBTQ+ employment rights, and broader human rights in general as a modern development, in reality thousands of people have been campaigning these issues for longer than most people anticipate.

For example, the first documented gay rights organisation

in the US, The Society of Human Rights, was founded in Chicago in 1925 by Henry Gerber. This pioneering organisation was awarded an official State of Illinois Charter, an acknowledgement to its significance. Gerber was inspired by the German Scientific-Humanitarian Committee, established in 1897, which he'd found out about while fighting in Germany during the war. It was eventually dissolved by the Nazis in 1933, despite being the oldest gay rights organisation in the world. Gerber created the first American publication for gay men called *Friendship and Freedom*, but a few months after the organisation's establishment, its members were rounded up and arrested on obscenity charges. Even though the charges were dropped, Gerber was dismissed from his job at the US Postal Service, and the legal fees incurred bankrupted him. Dale Jennings, inspired by the bravery of Gerber and his colleagues, set up a new organisation called the Mattachine Foundation in 1950, an inspirational organisation that would go on to encourage a wave of early gay rights organisations to rise up. The Los Angeles chapter, which extended inclusivity, welcomed women too. To keep members informed and connected, the chapter sent out a regular magazine, but the postal authorities seized them, refusing to post them to their intended subscribers. The US Post Office, continuing their early twentieth century reputation of being generally repressive, refused to deliver magazines for One Inc, calling them 'obscene', even though they were posted in paper envelopes no-one could see through. The organisation sued them, eventually winning the landmark victory lawsuit against them in the Supreme Court in 1958. In a significant turn of events, the court determined that 'material aimed at a gay audience was not inherently obscene'. It wasn't until 1975 before the proposal for the first bill to ban discrimination on the grounds of sexual orientation was introduced, but the Judiciary Committee barely looked at it before they dismissed it. One of the hardest professions for LGBTQ+ people has always been the military. The struggles faced by LGBTQ+ individuals in the military continued to unfold. In 1975, a decorated Vietnam War veteran was dishonourably discharged after revealing to his commanding officers that he was gay. After a five-year battle through the courts, the judges ruled that the military was wrong to dismiss him, finding the veteran had been unfairly discriminated against due to his sexual orientation. The court's decision led to financial compensation. In 1993, to counter this hard-won victory, Bill Clinton lifted the ban on gay people serving in the military, implementing the infamous policy of 'Don't Ask, Don't Tell,' which allowed Queer military personnel to serve, as long as they remained silent about their sexual orientation. In the UK, the ban on gay, lesbian, and bisexual military personnel serving in the armed forces was finally lifted in 2000, following a European Court of Human Rights ruling from 1999. The court has decided that dismissing two Naval personnel because they were gay was a breach of their human rights.

The United States and the United Kingdom took significant steps towards LGBTQ+ equality in the 1980s and 1990s. In 1982, Wisconsin became the first US State to ban discrimination based on sexuality, and in 1996 in the UK a court found that a worker who was fired before undergoing gender reassignment surgery was wrongfully dismissed. This case marked the first time that a court protected transgender people from employment discrimination. In the UK, the Employment

Equality (Sexual Orientation) Regulations in 2003 made it illegal to discriminate against gay, lesbian, and bisexual people in the workplace. Transgender people received equal protection under the Gender Recognition Act in 2004. Yet despite these advancements, in twenty-nine States of America it is still legal to fire people based on their sexuality, and in thirty-two states Transgender individuals can be dismissed for their gender identity.

Barbara Jordan's personal life was no secret to those around her. While she never publicly disclosed her sexual orientation, she never tried to hide it. Even when they bought 5 acres of land and built their own home, they would claim to outsiders they were close friends. In 1966, after her two failures at being elected to the House of Representatives, she decided to switch focus and campaigned to be elected to the Texas Senate. By 1966, Jordan sensed the political landscape had changed since her previous attempts. A series of landmark court cases had legally clarified the need for all residents to have equal representation, and how vital it was to eliminate gerrymandering. Gerrymandering was a common result of the end of racist segregation policies. With African Americans and other non-white groups now granted the right to vote as everyone else did, political leaders recognised the potential to manipulate the electoral landscape. By crafting voting district boundaries very carefully, they could consolidate most Black voters in a small number of districts, restricting the influence of their vote. As a result of the redrawing of certain districts in Texas, Barbara Jordan ran for the newly created 11th District. With new district borders, she won the election, becoming the first African American woman to join the Texas Senate, and the first Black Senator since her own great-grandfather, Edward Patton, represented the state in the House of Representatives in 1883. Moreover, her groundbreaking achievement was further recognised as the first LGBTQ+ woman in Congress.

During her two terms as a Senator, Jordan was a prolific legislator, authoring well over seventy different bills, primarily on subjects like anti-discrimination, the environment and governmental assistance for vulnerable populations. She campaigned for an increased minimum wage and greater financial compensation for people who were injured while on the job. She co-sponsored bills which increased pay for teachers and paid employers for hiring Disabled workers to boost employment numbers amongst those with impairments. She was incredibly popular across party lines for her commitment to the rules of the House and its processes, and she was frequently consulted on matters of procedure and law. She was knowledgeable but unafraid to ask advice, which endeared her to many individuals who were accustomed to the inflated egos of politicians who refused to consider being wrong. However, some critics from the Black community felt that she compromised her beliefs by accommodating smaller changes, rather than stand firm on hers to be made. In an interview she explained that '"the man" as many of our people call him, writes his books and knows the rules and makes the decisions. And so, I decided… it was necessary to find the door for getting inside just a little bit to find out what "the man" is doing, and how he acts and how he thinks.' In 1967, Lyndon B. Johnson, who had become president after the assassination of John F. Kennedy in 1963, took notice of Barbara Jordan's impressive work in the Senate. He was particularly impressed by her blend of talent and dedication and called Barbara Jordan to invite her to the White House. He was a big fan of Jordan, saying that 'wherever she goes, she's going to be at the top'. At the time, he was planning on introducing a civil rights section to the Fair Housing Act of 1967 and wanted to share the details with her first. When he was asked why Barbara, a relatively new addition to the Senate, should be invited he supposedly said, 'this is the brightest person in the State of Texas. ...She's got more common sense, more brains in her pinky than all these guys have from Harvard Business School and from all their corporations and Wall Street.' Jordan continued to think about her next step. She considered a seat in the House of Representatives but was advised to only pursue it if she was certain of winning. This would involve her moving out of Texas and representing her people in the capital, Washington DC, which naturally made her nervous, but she was confident she could make a tangible difference. During her campaign, Jordan would often say, 'I'll only be one of 435. But the 434 will know I'm there.' As she campaigned, Jordan experienced an unexpected honour, as part of a Texas tradition where the Governor and Deputy Governor take a day off to allow for someone to become an honorary Governor for a day, Jordan became the first Black woman to be Governor of a state and the first African American to ever preside over Texas. In a statement at the time, she said, 'I want you to celebrate this day as a new day of new commitment, when a new idea and a new sense of future is to be born in Texas'. Her family were so proud of her achievements, even her strict father, who had driven her so hard as a child, supposedly cried at the sight of her taking the reins of their home state. Despite his frail health, he was present for this momentous occasion. However later that day, after the ceremony, he collapsed and was taken to hospital, where he would sadly pass away the next day.

Barbara won her House of Representatives election and became the first woman elected in her own right to represent Texas. The support of former president Lyndon B. Johnson, who held significant influence, and now a friend, allowed her to join the House Judiciary Committee. It would take a few years before Barbara truly rose to public prominence. In the meantime, she threw herself into work and became well known in the House for her tireless dedication and ability to get things done.

As the Watergate scandal unfolded, it was more than just another political talking point. In anticipation of his re-election campaign, President Nixon ordered the headquarters of the Democratic Party to be broken into, and bugged, a move both illegal and morally reprehensible. An informant working with him began to pass information to journalists, knowing it was illegal. While Nixon and other important government figures denied all claims, they also withheld documents and recordings from the official investigators. Several people were arrested and charged with the crimes, but it was later revealed that the President and his aides had been bribing their co-conspirators to say that the President had no involvement in the scandal. Despite the evidence of his administration's wrongdoing, President Nixon still won another election. However, the scandal continued, and during the trial of one of the arrested burglars he suddenly confessed and admitted to the conspiracy. Everyone was caught off guard, and as result, a Senate Select Committee on Presidential Campaign Activities was opened. The committee was tasked with investigating whether President Nixon's actions warranted impeachment and whether he should be formally charged with misconduct. Barbara Jordan's rise to prominence during the Watergate hearings was a testament to her talent for public speaking. As a 'Freshman' Congresswoman, she could never have imagined the pivotal role she played in the impeachment inquiry, making her one of the most memorable speakers at the hearings. Despite being the last of the thirty-eight Congress members to speak, her speech, 'Statement on the Articles of Impeachment,' has since become known as one of the best and most mesmerising speeches in American history. While the Democrats had already secured the necessary votes to impeach Nixon from the forming of the committee, she pleaded with her colleagues to take their responsibility seriously and to do their research without rushing to judgement.. She spoke in defence and support of the Constitution, even though 'when that document was completed on 17 September 1787, I was not included in the "We, the people."' She said that even with all the faults at its creation, 'my faith in the Constitution is whole, it is complete, it is total'. She went through the impeachment criteria from the constitution's drafters and the current evidence against the President, noting that while they didn't yet know everything, said that 'if the impeachment provision in the Constitution of the United States will not reach the offenses charged here, then perhaps that eighteenth-century Constitution should be abandoned to a twentieth-century paper shredder!' When the Senate Hearings ended, Nixon went on TV to accuse the Committee of becoming 'increasingly absorbed to implicate the President personally in the illegal activities that took place'. Which I'm sure went down well with everybody on the Committee and really endeared him to them after all their hard work to examine the evidence fairly. At the end of July, the Committee voted on three 'articles of impeachment', or in other words, charges. These charges were obstruction of justice, misuse of power and contempt of Congress. But before the vote could be carried out in the House of Representatives, where a vote of agreement would have forced him out of office, Nixon resigned – meaning he was never technically impeached.

During her term as a Congresswoman, Barbara Jordan had been diagnosed with Multiple Sclerosis, an immune disorder that affects the nervous system, and caused lesions on the brain and damage to the nerves. She had tried to hide this as much as possible, but rumours about her illness and physical capabilities might have ended her chances of becoming attorney general. While she used a walking stick, and eventually a wheelchair, she would tell people it was due to a 'a bum knee' rather than the truth. It wasn't until she nearly drowned in a swimming pool in 1994 that she admitted her diagnosis of MS over twenty years before. The assumption for most people was that a Disability would end work opportunities, whether through physical incapacity or through the employer's assumptions that an employee could no longer complete the tasks given. In the US, before the Americans with Disabilities Act and Rehabilitation Act, it was a difficult struggle to find any job at all let alone keep it if you were Disabled. The National League of the Blind was formed in the UK in 1894, and fought against the tyranny that existed in the charity factories they were forced to work in. These factory workers did menial repetitive work and were staffed exclusively by Disabled people who were unable to find employment elsewhere. To receive a wage, even the low one paid by the factories, the charities dictated who married and who did not, they further prevented their workers from gaining any additional education. The National League of the Blind marched on the House of Commons and refused to leave until they had gained a new bill to support them. This early example of direct action may have inspired the League of the Physically Handicapped. They were set up in 1935 to protest the actions of the Works Progress Administration, an agency that employed people looking for jobs to build new roads and public buildings. The WPA, on receiving an application from a Disabled person, would stamp the applicant with the letters 'PH', meaning physically handicapped, and deny them access to the jobs being offered. Members staged a sit-in at their offices, refusing to leave for nine days, until they'd agreed to create 1,500 jobs for Disabled jobseekers. They didn't stop there. In 1942, the American Federation of the Physically Handicapped became the first pan-impairment political organisation to specifically lobby for an end to job discrimination. While the Civilian Vocational Rehabilitation Act had been passed by Congress in 1920, which expanded veteran rehabilitation programmes to civilians too. The Federation convinced the government that many of the vital jobs left behind during the Second World War because men went to fight, could be adequately filled by Disabled workers. The American Federation also successfully convinced the government to create a survey of the accessible job opportunities that were available in the federal government and established the National Employ the Physically

Handicapped Week. By 1962 the survey's name included those with Disabilities that weren't physical, and by 1988 the week became a month long event. Most of the future employment laws for Disabled people in the USA would be variations of the same Rehabilitation Act from 1920, but with additional amendments, inclusions, and exceptions. This includes the 1973 Rehabilitation Act, made famous by Section 504 and the sit-in it produced. By not revealing her impairment, Barbara was able to continue working with the aid of an assistant. While hiding her impairment, she fought for many issues, like voting reform and civil rights, but was forced to publicly refuse federal gay rights legislation so that she wouldn't make her sexuality too obvious. She said that 'there is no way that I can equate discrimination on the basis of sexual preference with discrimination on the basis of skin colour'. Many at the time, unaware that she was gay, thought she didn't understand homosexuality, having not experienced it. However, her viewpoint is in keeping with modern understandings of intersectionality, which is that discrimination against someone based on their race, sexuality, gender or disability isn't the same and can't be compared, and that by even trying to, you discriminate against individuals who have experienced multiple forms of discrimination. She was an obvious choice for the keynote speaker address at the Democratic National Convention in 1976. Her name had been linked as a possible nominee for the Supreme Court, Solicitor General or Attorney General, but what many sources call 'cruel rumours' ended that possibility. Those 'cruel rumours' were about her disability, and how could she possibly manage such a high-profile job? She became the first African American woman to give a keynote speech at the Democratic National

Convention and drew the attention of the crowd which even the previous speaker, the astronaut John Glenn, hadn't managed.

In 1979, she decided not to seek re-election and used the opportunity to return to Texas. She was employed in the public affairs department of the University of Texas, the same university that refused to admit her because she was Black. Her fascinating and engaging classes were so popular the university had to run a lottery for seats because so many students wanted to join her lectures. She was invited to the Democratic National Convention in 1992 as a keynote speaker, where Bill Clinton was nominated as the Democratic presidential candidate. She spoke from a wheelchair, and Clinton was so impressed that he wanted to nominate her for the Supreme Court, but unfortunately it was clear that her health would make that impossible. She did a lot of work in her later years on immigration reform, but soon slowed down to allow her body to rest, and enjoy a life of quality and quiet.

She became more ill, from both the effects of her Multiple Sclerosis and a recent diagnosis of leukaemia. Her partner Nancy cared for her, and she continued working with the university, politicians and her many other causes for as long as possible. When she died in 1995 of pneumonia related to her leukaemia diagnosis, Nancy continued to honour Barbara's desire for her private relationship to stay private and told the newspapers they were good friends and companions, but that 'people can say whatever they want'. Her death was devastating for the staff and students at University of Texas. Since working as a professor, she had become synonymous with the institution, and it held a memorial march in her honour. Bill Clinton declared a national time of mourning, and after her funeral she was buried in the Texas State Cemetery; the first

African American to receive the honour. As the former White House Press Secretary Bill Moyers said at her memorial, 'just when we despaired of finding a hero, she showed up, to give the sign of democracy'. Not bad for a woman who the *Houston Chronicle* declared was 'as cozy as a pile driver'.

Dr John Fryer

'You may take this as a declaration of war'

John Fryer was a high achiever from the moment he was born. Growing up in Winchester, Kentucky, he was in the second grade of elementary school two years early, at five years old. He completed high school at just fifteen, and at nineteen had finished studying for his bachelor's degree and graduated from university. As was inevitable, Fryer, a child prodigy, decided to attend medical school, and studied at Vanderbilt University in Nashville, Tennessee, graduating with his medical degree in 1962, and completing his medical internship at Ohio State University. As his specialty, he pursued psychiatry, and began his residency at Menninger Foundation in Topeka, Kansas. However, he became deeply unhappy. He began seeing a psychoanalyst who diagnosed him with Clinical Depression. The idea of a working psychiatrist needing psychiatric care himself was unthinkable, and so on the advice of his doctor he left the Menninger Foundation, and never told his patients or colleagues about his mental illness. However, John Fryer is not the only psychiatrist or mental health professional to live with ongoing mental illness – to the surprise of many, who assume to this day that a mental health professional would be unable to treat mental health conditions in others, while having one concurrently. Sigmund Freud is one famous example of a psychiatrist who not only lived with chronic depression but used it to further understand the depression of his patients, and develop new theories to treat it.

Technically, it was forbidden for homosexuals to practice psychiatry at all, and John Fryer knew that. He had read the literature. He'd seen the research and sat through lectures. 'So from the very beginning, I learned that it was pathology. And it was very difficult to get over that.' He later attributed his chronic depression to this internalised homophobia, compounded by hiding his homosexuality from everyone he worked with. The foundation he worked at was very homophobic, and to consider revealing his sexuality was not an option. He had no choice but to leave his job. To complete his residency, he uprooted his life and moved to a new facility twice more. First, to Philadelphia, where he held a residency at the University of Pennsylvania. But due to his sexuality and his slightly camp mannerisms, he was forced out again. He was left alone for long enough to complete his residency at Norristown State Hospital in 1967.

Following his residency he found a permanent job giving him time to dedicate to helping people in a similar situation to him. Since the mid-1960s, he had received referrals from the George W. Henry Foundation, which was founded in 1948 to help those 'who by reason of sexual deviation are in trouble with themselves, the law, or society'. The purpose of this foundation was to treat arrested homosexual men who were going through a court trial based on their sexuality. The men gave testimony and Dr. John Fryer testified on their behalf to the judges and jury that they were of good character. In 1967, he joined the Temple University in Philadelphia, as an instructor in psychiatry. He worked in the community health centre in North Philadelphia, becoming interested in the study of death and bereavement, and how it affected people psychologically. He dedicated most of his professional career to this, despite his notable work on homosexuality, and using a $5,000 grant from the Health Care and Human Values Task Force, he created a group dealing with matters concerning professional reactions to death and dying, calling it 'Ars Moriendi', Latin for The Art of Dying. This later became known as the International Work Group on Death, Dying, and Bereavement.

John applied for jobs at a variety of universities and hospitals, but internal gossiping ensured the rumours of his sexuality followed him wherever he went, and so he was turned away. More than anything, John wanted to teach. And he didn't want to jeopardise his ability to attain a faculty position. This fear was real, as homosexuality was listed as a psychiatric illness in the Diagnostic and Statistical Manual of Mental Disorders. Many hospitals didn't want a doctor with a diagnosable mental illness treating mentally ill patients.

The *Diagnostic and Statistical Manual of Mental Disorders* (or DSM) is a publication by the American Psychiatric Association which is used for the classification of mental disorders using a standard criterion for the diagnosis and treatment of mental illnesses. Four years prior to the publication of the first ever manual, the first Kinsey Report was published by zoologist Alfred Kinsey, and his fellow researchers. These reports became two bestselling books, *Sexual Behavior in the Human Male* in 1948, and *Sexual Behavior in the Human Female* in 1953. These books were immediately controversial, both within the scientific community and the public, because the research and the hypothesis published in the books challenged everyone's conventional beliefs about sexuality. It also discussed subjects previously only ever mentioned in hushed tones amongst trusted friends. The general finding of these reports was that 'only 50 per cent of the adult population is exclusively heterosexual throughout its adult life'. Whether this was because they were bisexual or had 'just experimented' with people of the same sex, research was based on a study of 5,300 men and 6,000 women, arguably who were recruited via methods that would ensure a higher representation of those with experience of same sex relationships. More rescarchers believe that Kinsey probably overestimated the rate of same-sex attraction because of these flaws in his sampling methods, but even so the thought that same sex attraction wasn't a niche subculture was a surprise to most. The psychiatry field in general was extremely hostile to the Kinsey Report, and the implication that same-sex sexual behaviour was far more common than mainstream society had previously believed. Nonetheless, his work is considered pioneering and some of the best-known sex research of all time and proved that homosexual acts were much more common than a lot of people had ever considered. In 1957, psychologist Evelyn Hooker published the results of a study that investigated the happiness of thirty self-identified homosexual men, in addition to a metric which measured how well adjusted they were, and compared it with the results from thirty heterosexual men. The conclusion that there was no difference between the two groups, being homosexual had no psychological bearing on someone's happiness and wellbeing, was staggering to many people at the time, and was a finding which stunned the medical community. The fore-runner to the DSM was the *Statistical Manual for the Use of Institutions of the Insane*, which was first published in 1918. This first *Statistical Manual* was ambiguous on the topic of homosexuality. It included a diagnosable condition, called 'constitutional psychopathic inferiority (without psychosis)', that was described as 'a large group of pathological personalities' including 'sexual perversions' but at no point specified that homosexual relations and desires were among them (although it was very much implied). By the time the first full DSM was published in 1952, homosexuality had been named as a mental illness, and classified within the larger 'sociopathic personality disturbance' category of personality disorders as a 'sexual deviation'. The sexual deviation diagnosis also included 'transvestitism, paedophilia, fetishism and sexual sadism' as examples. In the second edition of the DSM, published in 1968, the 'sexual deviation' diagnostic category was expanded with the larger category of 'personality disorders and certain other non-psychotic mental disorders', so that different 'sexual deviations' were listed under ten individual diagnostic codes.

'Codes' refer to the classifications of all recognised mental health disorders. While there was some question regarding whether homosexuality constituted a mental condition in the DSM-I and its predecessor, the Statistical Manual, the DSM-II removed any ambiguity that might have explicitly referred to homosexuality and the other 'sexual deviations' as mental disorders. While the DSM is used as a standard for diagnosis of various mental health conditions, its classification of homosexuality and other Queer identities as mental illnesses is far from the only criticism the manual has received over the years.

The fight against the American Psychiatrists Association for classifying normal sexuality as an illness, was conducted a long time before the association finally accepted they should act. An APA event in San Francisco covering the topic of aversion therapy, an appalling therapy that attempted to 'cure' homosexuality by making people associate their homosexual attraction with nausea, attempting to further legitimise what we now understand to be a torturous conversion therapy. Gay activists used this event to stand and stage a protest against the association and its stance that homosexuality was a mental illness that needed to be, cured. According to lesbian activist Barbara Gittings, the message of this protest was 'stop talking about us and start talking with us', bearing a striking similarity to the Disabled people's movement's famous protest slogan of 'nothing about us without us'. This protest was a great success, earning gay and lesbian activists a voice amongst the members of the association, and at their events. Their point of view and rebuttals of commonly held beliefs began to be sought out. At their Washington convention the following year, Gittings organised a panel discussion on the subject of 'Lifestyles of Non-patient Homosexuals', which was moderated by a gay astronomer from Harvard University named Dr Franklin E. Kameny. He had previously lost his job with the federal government purely because of his sexual orientation.

In 1964 Kameny went on national television and stated that being gay was 'not a disease, a pathology, a sickness, a malfunction, or a disorder of any kind'. He had actively opposed the psychological diagnosis of homosexuality, and consistently and openly campaigned on behalf of both closeted and freely gay people. In a piece for the medical magazine *Psychiatric News*, he claimed that the gay community 'object[s] to the sickness theory of homosexuality... based as it is on poor science'. Working with the Gay Liberation Front, who were formed immediately after the Stonewall Riots to campaign for gay rights, Kameny had planned a protest to demonstrate against the 1971 convention. Perhaps not the most elegant protest. He ran on stage, grabbed the microphone and shouted: 'Psychiatry is the enemy incarnate. Psychiatry has waged a relentless war of extermination against us. You may take this as a declaration of war against you'. At first, most of the APA, including the gay members, were frustrated and mildly irritated by this protest rather than angry. Fryer said, 'I frankly, at the beginning, remember the sense that I was embarrassed by it and that I wished they'd shut up. None of us were there'. They rolled their eyes at the folly of youth, never truly believing the definition of homosexuality would be changed. They saw it as nothing but a fool's errand, and a potentially dangerous reminder that there were far more gay people than they imagined. They believed this action ran the risk of giving the APA the ammunition to double down on patients and to crush the budding gay rights movement, but also placed gay psychiatrists at further risk of being outed and ostracised.

Following this demonstration, the APA decided to hold a discussion on homosexuality and mental illness at their annual meeting the following year. It included Kameny and Barbara Gittings on a panel titled 'Psychiatry: Friend or Foe to the Homosexual; A Dialogue'. Gittings went out looking for a gay psychiatrist who would be a part of the panel after his partner, Kay Lahusen, pointed out that while they had successfully represented both psychiatrists and homosexuals on the panel separately, there were no homosexual psychiatrists to fully appreciate the nature of the debate and save everyone from essentially guessing what it was like and what needed to be done. Considering no gay psychiatrists were willing to be publicly identified, she decided to take a different tack and instead read letters from homosexual psychiatrists without exposing their names, as no one would publicly talk to the Association. Barbara Gittings decided to contact Fryer and somehow persuaded him to show up. 'My first reaction was, no way. But she planted in my mind the possibility that I could do something and that I could do something that would be helpful, without ruining my career.' When he talked about this decision later in his life, he explained that his father's recent death and the grief and emotional upheaval associated with it prompted him to take that risk, but also made it very clear that he never would have agreed to be identifiable. It was only when Gittings suggested that he could wear a disguise for the entire event that he agreed to take part. Listed in the programme as just 'Dr H. Anonymous', with later lore extending the character's name to

'Dr Henry Anonymous' to add a bit of extra flavour, Fryer got to work on his secret disguise. 'My friend, who was in drama, and I talked about what the most effective disguise might be. And you may or may not know this, but if you wear clothes that are much too large for you, you look much smaller than you are. So, we decided to rent a large and very flamboyant tuxedo. We then decided that the best way to do my head was an over the head rubber mask. It was a Nixon mask that we distorted, so that you couldn't even see it was Nixon.' When the day of the event arrived, they waited until the last minute to sneak in the anonymous doctor, in a stretched plastic mask and a wide necked suit looking like a horror movie villain. In more recent years the sheer impact of his decision to speak publicly in that setting, even with a disguise, has been recognised and celebrated. 'The fact that someone would get up on stage, even in disguise, at the risk of professional denunciation or loss of job, was not a small thing. Even in disguise, it was a very, very brave thing to do.' At the time of his speaking at this event, Fryer was on the faculty of Temple University, but didn't have the security of tenure. Tenure is the prize that all academics and lecturers in the US strive for. It gives job security and academic freedom and can only be terminated under extraordinary circumstances. Much like his previous workplaces and at the Friends hospital where he was forced to leave due to his 'flamboyance', he was in real danger of losing his current position if he had been identified. He had been told by one University administrator that 'if you were gay and not flamboyant, we would keep you. If you were flamboyant and not gay, we would keep you. But since you are both gay and flamboyant, we cannot keep you'. Amazingly, despite this strong view and personal connection, that administrator never realised that 'Dr Anonymous' was Fryer, even while sitting in the front row at the 1972 event. He did however have some extra help with the disguise, a voice changer. In a slightly otherworldly tone, he announced to the assembled crowd 'I am a homosexual. I am a psychiatrist... I can assure you that I could be any one of more than 200 psychiatrists registered at this convention'. Shock rippled around the room; the other psychiatrists couldn't believe that there were so many homosexual members they didn't know about in the APA. He continued, explaining to them that 'as homosexuals who are psychiatrists, we seem to possess a unique ability to marry ourselves to institutions rather than wives or lovers. Many of us work twenty hours daily to protect institutions who would literally chew us up and spit us out if they only knew'. The assembled doctors fell silent as he methodically but openly described the risks of being a practising psychiatrist and psychoanalyst in a deeply homophobic speciality. He described how they were 'required to be more "healthy" than their heterosexual counterparts' to make up for the fact that they were gay and, God forbid, flamboyant. He also described how psychiatrists were, maybe understandably, shunned in the gay community since they had the power to declare their peers were mentally ill for sharing the same sexuality as them. 'As psychiatrists who are homosexual, we must look carefully at the power which lies in our hands to define the health of others around us'. He described how the many gay psychiatrists in the APA had to spend their lives hiding their sexuality from their fellow workers as they were terrified of the very real possibility of discrimination. But they were also fearful of revealing their profession to fellow homosexuals owing to the understandable disdain in which the psychiatric profession was held among the gay community. Fryer's speech was novel, he spoke directly to the gay members in the audience, and suggested ways in which homosexual psychiatrists could subtly and 'creatively' challenge the prejudice which was found in their profession in a way which meant they didn't have to disclose their sexuality. He also considered how they could help their gay patients survive in a world that considered their sexual orientation a psychological disease. While he was at significant risk by speaking out, and potentially being outed professionally, he later said that he realised that the whole community was 'taking an even bigger risk, however, in not living fully our humanity, with all the lessons it must teach all the other humans around us. This is the greatest loss, our honest humanity, and that loss leads all those others around us to lose that little bit of their humanity as well'. Incredibly, Fryer and Kameny weren't alone in their assertion that the APA was incorrect. In a turn of events considered unthinkable even a few years before, Dr Judd Marmor, at the time the APA's vice president and soon to be its president, said after Dr Anonymous' speech that, 'I must concede that psychiatry is prejudiced as has been charged. Psychiatric mores reflect the predominant social mores of the culture'. He later wrote to explain his viewpoint that, 'in a democratic society we recognise the rights of such individuals to have widely divergent religious preferences, if they do not attempt to force their beliefs on others who do not share them'. He said that while he considered the issues similar, that the 'attitudes toward divergent sexual preferences, however, are quite different, obviously because moral values – couched in 'medical' and 'scientific' rationalisations – are involved'.

Straight after the panel event, Fryer was whisked away to a local radio station. There, as 'Dr Anonymous' he spent two hours discussing his experiences as a gay psychiatrist, and answered questions about how the APA could fix the problems that they had caused. His radio segment was played out live from a local gay bar. Even though he used a voice changer on stage and on the radio, it was an open secret among many gay psychiatrists who Dr H. Anonymous was. Several colleagues knew it was him, but he didn't openly admit to being the anonymous gay psychiatrist until 1994.

While the idea of homosexuality was becoming more accepted, it still took convincing to make any kind of official change. The DSM committee believed that homosexuality was in fact a mental disorder that belonged in the DSM, but after their technical advisor started having meetings with gay activists, including the secret group of gay APA members that Fryer was a member of, who later became the Association of Gay and Lesbian Psychiatrists, he began to see another viewpoint. He went in search of more data and after reviewing the work of researchers like Kinsey, he had a change of heart. The culmination of this work was the development of a proposal to potentially remove homosexuality from the DSM, and instead replace it with a more specific 'sexual orientation disturbance'. The amendment featured in the proposal was eventually accepted after a vote by the board of trustees for the American Psychiatric Association at the end of 1973 and was approved by the entire APA membership at the next conference in 1974. The previous diagnostic 'code' assigned to gayness was then given a brand-new identity in the DSM-II's seventh printing in 1974. The rebranding of 'homosexuality' to a 'sexual orientation disturbance' added some extra information that clarified the new definition: homosexuality 'by itself does not constitute a psychiatric disorder'. Instead, the diagnosis of this 'sexual orientation disturbance' should be used only for patients who 'are either disturbed by, in conflict with, or wish to change their sexual orientation'. There was one person, called Spitzer, who insisted that the DSM couldn't remove homosexuality entirely, and it still had to include a specific diagnosis for homosexuals who were distressed by their sexuality, rather than just considering it a form of another existing mental illness such as depression or anxiety. Several psychiatrists, including those who had previously argued vehemently in favour of declassifying homosexuality as a mental disorder, publicly resigned from the APA committee which consulted on the DSM. Spitzer's determination to include this additional diagnosis was seen by many people as an attempt to maintain the status quo and continue to claim that homosexuality was a disease, by saying that a person acting on their sexuality was an act of distress.

Soon after the release of this new addition of the DSM, the governing body of the American Psychiatric Association issued a novel and startling position statement, far removed from their previous stance. It called for private sexual acts between consenting adults to be decriminalised and for an end to anti-homosexual prejudice amongst the psychiatric community, and the public in general. However, even while they were stating this, the APA made it clear that it did not agree with the notion that homosexuality was a normal and typical sexual variation. They went back on their claim that they wanted to end homophobia.

This sudden change of classification and stance prompted the

Philadelphia Bulletin to print the very funny and slightly sarcastic headline 'Homosexuals gain instant cure'. Fryer's influence in this decision was obvious at the time, and his speech has since been cited as a direct and key factor in finally persuading the psychiatric community to do the right thing and publicly reach this decision. Gittings later said of it: 'His speech shook up psychiatry. He was the right person at the right time'. In a 1985 issue of the newsletter of the Association of Gay and Lesbian Psychiatrists, Fryer wrote that he believed that it was 'something that had to be done' and 'the central event in my career... I had been thrown out of a residency because I was gay. I lost a job because I was gay... It had to be said, but I couldn't do it as me... I was not yet full time on the [Temple] faculty'. After his speech, and after the DSM changed its classifications, he noted the drastic changes. 'I am now tenured, and tenured by a chairman who knows I'm gay. That's how things have changed.'

Ironically, since the removal of homosexuality from the DSM, the protests haven't stopped. APA meetings have been disrupted by 'ex-gay' activists, those who claim to have been cured of their homosexuality, wanting the psychiatrists to change their minds again to state that homosexuality is a mental illness, and make conversion therapy available for every gay person. According to Drescher: 'Every year, we get a group of people who ... ask for homosexuality to be put back in the manual... They're, interestingly, the only group who does it. Every other group wants their diagnoses taken out; they want theirs back in'.

After this whole saga, Fryer returned to his regular life, practising psychiatry quietly. He became a professor at Temple

University, both of psychiatry, and of family and community medicine. He specialised in the treatment of drug and alcohol addiction as well as focusing on grief, death, and bereavement for dying people and their families and loved ones. Later in his career, with the AIDS crisis raging amongst his community, he treated gay men with AIDS who faced their own deaths. He would treat them in his home office rather than in his practice at Temple, as he openly treated gay men, and so many of them could have been outed if spotted at his main clinic. He was paramount in the founding of several organisations, including the Philadelphia AIDS Task Force, Temple's Family Life Development Center, the APA International Work Group on Death, Dying, and Bereavement, and Physicians in Transition. He was committed to educating psychiatrists and other doctors on grief and bereavement and was a vital figure in restructuring the help offered at several hospices both nearby home in Philadelphia, and much further afield in London, UK. While he retired in 2000, he was far from forgotten by his peers. He was given a 'Distinguished Alumnus' award by Vanderbilt University in 2002, and in the same year, he was given a Distinguished Service Award by the Association of Gay and Lesbian Psychiatrists (AGLP).

Fryer died in 2003 from a sudden and acute illness. He was memorialised by the American Psychiatric Association and the Association of Gay and Lesbian Psychiatrists who created the 'John E. Fryer, M.D. Award' in his honour. This was awarded to psychiatrists who had worked to improve the lives and mental health of those in sexual minorities. The first two winners of the award in 2006 were Barbara Gittings and Frank Kameny.

He will forever be remembered for the impact his actions had, and for the great personal and professional risk that he took to make things better for people like him. While his impairment may not seem like an obvious inclusion in this volume, his mental health was so profoundly affected by the discrimination in his life it must be part of the shared Disabled and Queer experience. His experience without doubt contributed to his decisions, and shows us that when multiple marginalisations may not be related, they intermingle in a way that can't be detangled.

Harriet Martineau

'Frightened on beholding the human face'

If you asked many individuals to name a famous sociologist today, most wouldn't be able to. Ask many people to even explain what sociology is and most would struggle. Arguably, the name Harriet Martineau used back then is clearer. At least we can get the gist of what 'political economy' is. But today, she is known by many as the first female sociologist, as well as one of the very few women who was able to make a living with her writing in the nineteenth century.

It was 1855 when Harriet Martineau started feeling a familiar pain in her chest. She assumed she was dying, and her top priority from then on was recording her life and legacy. The result remains to this day one of the most detailed autobiographies of a woman from this period. The fact that she lived another twenty-one years is beside the point.

Most women led unrecorded lives. Many in the past have assumed that unrecorded means unremarkable. But Harriet was far from it. She was incredibly popular in her time, with even the future Queen Victoria being a fan, to the point that Harriet was invited to her very, very long coronation. She had to stand the entire time but had at least prepared for the long breaks between all the pomp and good stuff. She reflected that, 'I had carried a book; and I read and ate a sandwich, leaning against my friendly pillar, till I felt refreshed' which I'm sure was exactly the impression Queen Victoria wanted to make with her coronation.

She was born on 12 June 1802 to a well-off family in Norwich, made up of surgeons, business owners and priests. She was the sixth of eight children, and she was partially Deaf from birth, and seen as a 'sickly' child. Having grown up with disabilities and chronic illness, she was experienced in the reactions of others to her ailments, and basically described the social model of disability, much earlier than we ever anticipate it being understood. She wrote that, 'We sufferers meet with abundance of compassion for our privations: but the privation is (judging by my own experience) a very inferior evil to the fatigue imposed by the obstruction'. In other words, people are sympathetic about our physical deprivation, but that physical deprivation is much less of a problem than the exhaustion caused by all the barriers. This bears a startling resemblance to the social model which, as we've seen, states that Disabled people are disabled by barriers in society rather than their medical impairment, and we should strive for a societal solution for our exclusion. The medical model however states that we are disabled by our impairments and should aim for a medical solution, but most people are now recognising the limitations of such a strict model.

The family was unitarian but progressive, and her father was a successful textile manufacturer running his own business as well as being a deacon of the local Chapel. Her mother was the daughter of a grocer and sugar refiner. She got used to being seen as 'the sick child' early in her youth and later in her life wrote of how she and her mother had a difficult relationship after she supposedly abandoned her to a wet nurse. The use of wet nurses for richer families was commonplace, and so whether she was literally abandoned we can't know for sure, but she certainly felt it. A series of dramas featuring the wet nurse seem to have been commonplace in Harriet's youth. Harriet's mother attributed all her medical woes to the fact that the wet nurse hired had been unable to provide enough milk to Harriet in the first few weeks of her life. Out of fear for her job and the wrath of her employers, she attempted to carry on regardless, long after she'd run out of milk, leaving Harriet undernourished. Martineau wasn't so sure about whether this was the cause or not, even though that's what her mother had repeatedly told her and put at least some of her symptoms down to milk 'radically disagreeing' with her. Lactose intolerance aside, she was sent to live in numerous places far away for her health as she was considered a 'delicate' child. She was frequently so severely anxious and panicky that she would experience periods of what we might now consider to be panic attacks. It is very hard to reverse diagnose people from the past and many specifically refrain from it for these reasons, making the study of disability very difficult, but from her own words in her autobiography, the descriptions match very closely. She describes her childhood self as 'usually very unhappy' and talks about contemplating suicide frequently, saying that she wanted to join God in Heaven. Due to her family's relatively liberal faith, she didn't see her death occurring by suicide as a potential barrier to her entry to heaven like many other denominations would. Harriet however believed that a decent amount of her problems wouldn't have existed at all if she had just had a more nurturing home environment. In her autobiography she describes her mother as quite cold and distanced, and not in any way naturally loving or affectionate. She says she was 7 years old by the time she could be convinced that some people did care about her. She was just 2 years old, still a toddler, when she was first sent away from home for her health. This was not unusual for families lucky enough to have connections in the countryside or by the sea. It was thought that fresh air would do a world of good, and possibly cure any ailment caused by the environment. Staying with a methodist family, she returned home having become something of a miniature preacher, proclaiming phrases seemingly at random like 'duty first, pleasure later' and making her own tiny books with all the sayings that she had learnt written inside.

When she was 3, her brother James was born, the seventh child of the Martineaus, who would go on to become Harriet's confidant and closest friend. It was he who eventually suggested she begin writing full time, to ease the separation when he went away to university as a young man, leaving her behind in the family home. Throughout her childhood she was repeatedly afflicted with frequent earache, which resulted in a gradual loss of her hearing, bringing her number of fully functioning senses down to two as she had never had a sense of smell or taste. Being unable to smell or taste anything didn't seem to affect her life in any way, unlike her impending Deafness.

Thanks to the family's more liberal religious denomination, all the Martineau girls received a conventional education, just like the boys. Although the women weren't trained to expect a career unlike the men of the house, they avoided having to settle for the domestic centred education that many from poorer families had to be content with. Due to Harriet's health issues, she was taught at home for the first few years which led to a certain amount of teasing from her siblings. While it was common for wealthy girls to be educated at home with a governess, in her family it was just Harriet who experienced this. She was taught French, Latin, maths and writing, partly by her parents, before transferring to a small religious school when she was around 9 years old.

She had long been interested in politics after witnessing the aftermath of the death of Admiral Nelson and developed a keen sense of social justice very young when she was forced to take rude messages from her family to the servants in her house. She despised the way the staff were treated by the well off. It just wasn't fair. That outrage never left her. The teacher at her school, Mr Perry was the one to truly kick start her fascination with learning, and interest in a wide range of other academic subjects. Her school years, though, were marred by her overwhelming self-consciousness, attributed to her Deafness, her poor handwriting and weirdly, her hair. After Mr Perry left the school in Norwich and left Harriet without a teacher who understood her, she tried to continue learning on her own despite her worsening deafness.

She notes in her autobiography several themes that many people will still recognise in the issues of Deaf education today. She wrote that she had 'never seen a deaf child's education well managed at home, or at an ordinary school. It does not seem to be ever considered by parents and teachers how much more is learned by oral intercourse than in any other way'. Thankfully there have been improvements in Deaf education since the dark days of the 1800 Milan Conference which decided that all Deaf children should be forced to communicate in verbal English, but there is much that still needs to be changed. She also had some insights into Deaf stereotypes which thankfully doesn't still go on to such a large degree. I certainly don't remember too often hearing that 'the deaf are sly and tricky, selfish and egotistical'.

At 16 she was sent to stay in Bristol for education and health, where her much loved aunt worked. She was happy there for the fifteen months she stayed, aside from some homesickness, and was able to spend time talking to and learning with her well read and educated cousins. She was significantly older than all the other girls in her classes, and her deafness was significant enough that by this time she really struggled in class. She was very self-conscious of her Deafness and was frustrated by people's responses to it. 'They blamed me for not doing what I was sorely tempted to do – inquiring of them about everything that was said, and not managing in their way, which would have made everything all right'.

As a result, for over a year, most of her education was done alone in private study. She loved the walks around Bristol and by the time she left, she was less fearful, more open to people and opportunities, with an even deeper relationship with her God and her religion, but much sicker. She was constantly frustrated by the idea that women were expected to just stay in the home, sewing and always ready to receive visitors. 'And thus [her] first studies in philosophy were carried on with great care and reserve', in secret from the rest of the family.

In 1821 she began writing anonymous articles for a Unitarian magazine called *Monthly Repository*. One of those articles, in 1823, was called 'On Female Education' and reflected on many of her experiences. Her brother and best friend advised that she should 'leave it to other women to make shirts and darn stockings and devote [herself] to this'. As was expected of any young woman in her position, she became engaged to a friend of her brother James, but their relationship was troubled. He had been significantly mentally ill, and he later died. While she was sort of upset that he had died, she was relieved that she had managed to get away with not marrying him. A major contributing factor to that could be that it is believed by many that Harriet was probably gay. She was known to have had several very close and profound relationships with women, often referred to as 'romantic friendships' although it's almost certain that she never acted upon these feelings physically. Of course, this is all a heavy dose of speculation based on how she talks and writes of women and men. Like the issues that come from reverse diagnosing historical figures with specific medical issues, concluding that historical figures were Queer is much debated. As well as this, she spoke publicly and openly of her support for contraception, sex work and divorce and examined her feelings of detachment from her gender in her book *Life in the Sick Room*. She saw infidelity as an inevitable side effect of people being forced into loveless monogamous marriages because they felt they had to, so it's safe to say her relationship with gender and sexuality was novel for its time. However, if all of that isn't enough to justify her entry in this book, I will add that according to the voters on VIPFAQ.com, 100 per cent of people believe that Harriet Martineau was gay. I rest my case.

After her father died in 1826, the family textile business went into a rapid decline. Understandably, without its founder and leader, it failed three years later. Harriet and her sisters had to go out and earn a living for themselves and help the family survive, rather than relying on the business' money as they had up until then. With her hearing loss, and the amount of noise children famously make, she would have been unsuitable as a governess which was the default for educated women of her class. Although she could have made a living with her very skilled needlework, she didn't need to, and as unlikely as it seemed for a woman, she was able to support herself with writing instead. A story she later wrote called *Berkeley the Banker* was based on this difficult experience and was said by those who knew about everything that had happened to be 'a pretty faithful account of the event'. Then Harriet had a brilliant idea. She wanted to write a series of books about political economy. Stories aimed at everyone to help them understand social justice issues. It was a hard sell though. Publishers didn't think ordinary people would be interested in such a thing. After a long period of battling for someone to take on the first book, she was eventually forced to accept very unfavourable terms to get it into print. Its immediate success surprised everyone and allowed her to move alone to the big city of London in 1832. She continued to write for the *Monthly Repository* while also publishing books about religion based on her beliefs and interpretations of the church. She then shifted permanently to what she is best known for: writing illustrative articles about political economy, a long-winded way of describing what we would often now call sociology – the study of social patterns, behaviour and interactions. She presented these as stories aimed at ordinary members of the community, who wouldn't have previously studied these topics which helped people to understand the various causes for social reform. Nobody had previously aimed their writing on this subject at this group before, and the timing was perfect. It was on everybody's minds since when the first edition came out the Great Reform Act Crisis was consuming the country.

Thanks to the popularity of this first edition, and the following full series of *Illustrations on Political Economy*, she was now financially secure and decided that since she had the money, she'd like to travel outside of England, and decided to travel around America for the next two years.

While the idea of going around Europe had piqued her interest, she was drawn to the USA by something a bit different from a standard jolly: to see how the new democratic principles were working over there. Although she also claimed that she wanted to 'rough it' for a while so I'm not sure how reliable her information on the country was. After she returned, no-one was in any doubt of her opinion on the place, as much of her following works were blistering critiques of how America had failed to live up to their aims for a new democracy. She was particularly critical of how they treated women, who she said were given 'indulgence rather than justice'. She was said to have had a romantic entanglement with her American friend Margaret Fuller, the first American female war correspondent and transcendentalist who wrote extensively on same sex love. However, they had a massive falling out, to the point that after Fuller's death Harriet said that she had 'shallow conceits' and 'looked down upon persons who acted instead of talking'. Speculation still bubbles that this falling out could have contributed to her strong negative feelings on the state of feminism in the USA, and maybe on the country. While she was already known by her friends and acquaintances to be an abolitionist, she was drawn into the anti-slavery cause and became close to the groups in America that campaigned for its abolition. It would remain a passion for the rest of her life.

Over the next few years, she then published two novels and a series of children's stories called the Playfellow series before finally relenting to the temptation and pressure of her friends' recommendations and travelled to Europe where she was when she fell ill in 1839. When it didn't quickly clear up, she travelled to Newcastle where her sister and brother-in-law, who was a doctor, lived. She and her sister had a good relationship, although not as close as her and James, and with her brother-in-law's connections she was diagnosed with ovarian cysts and a prolapsed uterus. She lived with them in Tynemouth bedbound for five years, after being told her condition was likely terminal. But then a friend suggested mesmerism. She was deeply sceptical of anything that could allegedly cure her so easily, as she had both a scientific mind and a deep religious belief. It took several months for her to be convinced to at least give it a go. Her own suspicion was compounded by the fact that her sister and brother-in-law were incredibly dismissive of the idea of mesmerism and didn't believe in it at all. However, in the end it was a letter from her youngest sister, whose husband (also a surgeon) had used mesmerism for pain relief during an operation, which convinced her to try it.

Mesmerism, or 'animal magnetism', is what we would call hypnotism now, and is where we get the term 'mesmerising' from. Mesmerism was used for the treatment of a wide range of physical and mental illnesses and ailments and had a significant influence on medicine throughout the romantic era. It was discovered by a doctor called Franz Mesmer, who naturally named his method after himself. After several sessions of this therapy, she was symptom free after so long. Naturally, she believed she was cured and that it was all thanks to mesmerism. She moved to the Lake District, building her own house, and starting immediate work on numerous new books and articles.

Mesmer had moved to Vienna in 1759 to study medicine. He primarily studied and worked on the influences of the planets on the human body, believing that tides could affect the human body just like the sea. This was the subject of his doctoral thesis, and also some other people's doctoral theses, as investigations have since determined that he definitely plagiarised at least some of it. In 1774, due to the eighteenth-century tradition of making sick people drink and eat things we would now determine to be poisonous (for example, mercury and radium), Mesmer had made a woman with hysteria drink some iron mixed into a solution. He thought he had had a breakthrough when he supposedly cured her, by using magnets that he pressed against her skin to drag the iron solution around and create an 'artificial tide' which she had felt moving around inside. His theory soon developed, which stated that all humans contained a magnetic fluid inside them, and that it was the blocking of this fluid within a range of channels across the body that caused disease. When the channels became unblocked, the patients would go into a brief 'crisis' and soon be relieved of their symptoms. Some people just couldn't control their magnetic fluid themselves and needed help to unblock their channels.

After a few experiments which proved that people didn't respond to magnets if they didn't know they were there (which damaged his reputation somewhat) he concluded that he must have contributed his own 'animal magnetism' which was what had caused the artificial tide of magnetic fluid to move. Not that Mesmer's practice was particularly new or innovative, it was like several processes that had been used by faith healers for centuries. Supposedly, his importance in the study of this type of healing is his insistence that the effects had a scientific basis. As a secular man and scientist, he clashed with people who claimed that his successes were miracles or reflective of any form of religion. Unlike the 'charlatans' that many had boxed him in with, Mesmer took part in numerous panels and experiments to prove the scientific basis behind his methods. These did not go well for him. Panel after panel performing experiment after experiment were unable to prove that this process worked at all. But none of this deterred Harriet. She was convinced, and it changed her opinions on several subjects. She published what is seen as her most controversial book, called *Letter on the Laws of Man's Nature and Development* in 1851. It rejected her former religious beliefs as well as publicised her belief in mesmerism, which fractured her relationship with her closest brother James, who by this point was a leading figure in the Unitarian Church. This marked a sudden change in Harriet, whose early life was defined by her religious principles. There was also speculation that James felt usurped as Harriet's hero figure as the relationship between the mesmerist and their patient was usually one of devotion and reverence. She had previously described him as her 'oracle', so the loss of her best friend from her life devastated her. It is said that Harriet was significantly more susceptible to female mesmerists than male, which is said by some to be yet more proof of her attachment to women, contradicting a 1977 essay which refutes the 'allegation' of lesbianism by claiming that Harriet would obviously be drawn to these interesting women only because she herself was 'plain' and a 'less than desirable commodity'. Her supposed cure by mesmerism also ended her warm relationship with her oldest sister and her husband, who she stayed with after first becoming unwell in Europe, as they had a natural prejudice. However, she later believed some of this change was due to her sister also being unwell, and in fact in the early stages of an illness that would eventually kill her.

In 1852 she started getting a regular pay cheque, for working at a newspaper that was imaginatively called the *Daily News* and wrote thousands of articles for them over the next sixteen years, as well as for other publications such as the *Edinburgh Review*. At this time, she also published new translations of classic texts by the philosopher Auguste Comte, and the fight to win women the right to vote in all British elections. While we recognise the names of a few famous suffragettes and suffragists, it's easy to forget that the bulk of why the campaign succeeded was because normal, everyday women jumped into the fray. Harriet had lived a symptom-free and painless life for several years, embracing her new-found health with work travel. However, after this long respite, she fell ill again in 1855.

The debate over the efficacy of mesmerism had been long raging, and not just around the family dinner table. While a Royal Commission is understood in the UK to refer to a public inquiry into a specific issue, two different Royal Commissions on Animal Magnetism in 1784 were used in France as a scientific trial into mesmerism. Mesmer had never stopped trying to prove the science behind his methods. He reluctantly agreed to a Royal Commission and took on many cases that seemed impossible, to try and show the world that he wasn't a charlatan. The best way to prove himself, he believed, would be to cure a seemingly incurable patient unequivocally and undeniably. Luckily, or unluckily for her, Maria Theresa Paradis was that patient. A pianist who had been blind since childhood, she had been unsuccessfully treated by many other doctors with methods such as electrocuting and putting leeches in her eyes which, incredibly, hadn't helped. After several sessions, Mesmer claimed he had been able to partially cure her, with her being 'frightened on beholding the human face', but this wasn't enough. There were rumours that their sessions had become less about the mental powers of suggestion and more about the two of them collaborating physically, in a sexy way. He was just so damn magnetic. Yet another doctor declared him a charlatan and Maria's father couldn't have people losing interest in his blind daughter and her lucrative piano playing. Maria just wanted everyone to leave her alone. And so, in 1778 he left for Paris, but the news travelled fast. The well-to-do of the city were split, between people who thought he was a fraudster and those who felt he'd been treated unfairly by a world that just didn't understand. However, there were still enough people who wanted his treatment that he had to start offering group therapy by way of a subscription fee.

He did this by way of what he called 'a baquet'. Essentially a giant wooden tub of water with metal rods sticking out of it would be in the centre of the floor, while the room was made ambient and relaxing with velvet everywhere, incense and low light. People would hold the rods, place them to the parts of their bodies needing treatment and eventually, after being touched by an assistant, fall into a state of laughter, screaming or fits which must have been startling at best. Once Mesmer arrived, he would touch his patients and they would be immediately released from their trance and cured.

Harriet had made her peace with the clear reality that this treatment wouldn't work for her a second time, whatever method her mesmerist used. She was so sure that she was dying, that she wrote the entire two volumes of her autobiography in three months. Even though she lived for another twenty-one years, these went completely unaltered. Maybe she thought she'd get round to it eventually, or maybe she feared that adding to it would encourage her to edit the earlier sections. And so, the final part was written relatively soon after she died by Maria Weston Chapman, an Abolitionist friend from America. She wrote of her (assumed) impending death that, 'I certainly feel no dislike or dread of it; nor do I find my pleasant daily life at all overshadowed by the certainty that it is near its end'. And of course, by 'certainty', she meant the exact opposite.

Although she officially retired in 1869, she continued to write for causes that were important to her. When the Contagious

Diseases Act was introduced in 1864, she wrote many articles attacking it. These laws allowed women who were suspected of being prostitutes to be detained and forcibly examined to test for venereal diseases. This was aimed at reducing venereal diseases in the armed forces. Naturally, Harriet believed that there was a much easier way to do this that didn't involve rounding up all the sex workers and helped form the National Association for the Repeal of the Contagious Diseases Acts. She detested the idea of any laws that applied exclusively to women.

These days, she is remembered as the first female sociologist, as well as the first person to even attempt to make the ideas of social justice and political economy accessible to the masses. While aimed at the less educated, its fans spanned social classes and income levels. The then young Princess Victoria was a big fan of her work, so much so that, 'a friend of mine who was at Kensington Palace one evening when my Political Economy series was coming to an end, told me how the Princess came, running and skipping, to show her mother the advertisement of the "Illustrations of Taxation", and to get leave to order them.' She also made herself an ongoing reputation in activism, campaigning for the abolition of slavery, women's rights, and the rights of other minority groups. Her autobiography is considered one of the best and most detailed autobiographies written by a woman in the nineteenth century, although there aren't really many others to challenge her title. Her impairments as a Deaf and chronically ill woman clearly contributed to her values, ideology and work, as did much of her, privileged upbringing.

When she died in 1876, an autopsy proved conclusively that the ovarian cyst that she believed had been cured by mesmerism, had in fact continued growing. It was more likely that all her ill health since 1855 had been caused by it. However, since she went ten years without feeling any symptoms of this significant ailment, quality of life-wise it clearly worked in some way. She had written in her autobiography after her first cure with mesmerism that, 'I could quote several medical men who reasoned that, as my disease was an incurable one, I could not possibly be radically better', but on seeing all the things she could now do, 'then the doctors said I had never been ill!' This just shows that doctors claiming to know it all is practically a historical tradition.

Despite the two French Royal Commissions Mesmer participated in (one of which was ordered by the Queen of France after he wrote to her asking for money) and a Royal Academy investigation both finding that while some sick people seemed to be cured by his methods, there was no evidence of any magnetic fluid inside people (shocker), many carried on Mesmer's practice and developed it. The newcomers almost immediately kicked the idea of magnetic fluid to the side but continued the practice of what they referred to as 'the power of suggestion' which they believed was the true source of symptom relief, but only when it was led by an experienced and charismatic person. But the controversy continued after Mesmer was gone. While in France and other parts of western Europe the debate between whether mesmerism was a huge cruel hoax or a miracle treatment for incurable patients was raging in public, in England it was mainly confined to the pages of journals and magazines. The best known of the Mesmeric journals was called *The Zoist* and was set up and edited by John Elliotson who was a progressive phrenologist. You may remember phrenology from such societal ills as racism, sexism, and eugenics. He had been expelled from University College Hospital for his use of mesmerism, although he was also the first in Britain to use a stethoscope and promoted acupuncture, so make of that what you will. He set up the journal as a source of first-hand accounts, case studies and general information and published several letters and accounts by Harriet herself. She wrote several excellent articles, such as 'Mesmeric Cure of a Cow' and the much-anticipated sequel 'Distressing effects in a Doctor upon the removal of a Disease from a Cow with Mesmerism'. During her break from symptomatic disease, she compiled the booklet *Letters on Mesmerism* which featured several first-hand accounts of mesmeric cures. These weren't enough to fend off the mockery of many people and satirical cartoons involving donkeys. The medical and scientific community would be helpless with laughter at these, the closest thing the nineteenth century had to memes. As time went on the scientists and doctors eventually accepted the benefits of mesmerism, much of it thanks to the work of the Scottish surgeon James Braid. Although soon enough, particularly in England, they referred to it almost exclusively as hypnotism (a term he coined) to try and distance itself from all that magnets and tide stuff. They concluded that its benefits were caused by the somnambulist state brought on by the power of suggestion and an individual patient's susceptibility. Put simply, if the patient believed that hypnosis could work for them, they could be put into a state that looked like a trance and told what they were thinking, until they were thinking it too.

In the mid-nineteenth century, Austrian physician Josef Breuer's work got attention for his treatment of Anna O for hysteria, that classic illness that as many of us know is essentially a synonym for 'diagnosed as a woman'. Breuer used suggestive hypnosis to trigger Anna's childhood emotions, which he said resulted in the reduction of her symptoms.

This wasn't the only experimentation with trying to alter the inner thoughts of someone's mind using hypnosis. Around the same time, Richard von Krafft-Ebing was testing out an early version of what we would now call conversion therapy. He is now credited by many as being the first to claim success in turning Queer people straight in the nineteenth century. He was the German psychiatrist and hypnotist who wrote the *Psychopathia Sexualis* (Sexual Psychopathy: A Clinical-Forensic Study) in 1886. This well-known dictionary of kink, fetish and sexuality was further expanded on until there were twelve editions and contained 238 case studies of what he determined was 'deviant sexual behaviour'. These books introduced to the English language terms such as 'sadist', 'masochist', 'homosexuality' and 'bisexuality'. While this was primarily focussed on men, some editions featured sections on female sexual deviancy and lesbian love, which was unusual for the time.

However, it wasn't just Krafft-Ebing who used hypnosis for the purpose of 'hetero-fying' members of the public, although this new guy had a better instinct for flare and flourish. In 1899, at a hypnosis conference, another psychiatrist faced the audience and declared, to their amazement, that he had turned a gay man straight. As Albert von Schrenck-Notzig told it, all it had taken were forty-five hypnosis sessions and a few trips to a brothel. To the rapt crowd he described how, using hypnosis and the power of suggestion, he had manipulated the man's sexual desire towards men and diverted it towards women. But Breuer wasn't alone in his belief of the unending possibilities of hypnosis, and Schrenck-Notzig wasn't the only one with theories on homosexuality. As the use of the power of suggestion became more widely familiar to the psychiatric profession, study into the mechanisms of how it worked led to further theories about the causes of several diseases, disorders and differences. A more famous colleague of Breuer was the neurologist Sigmund Freud. Using a method of hypnosis on his patients, Freud discovered the unconscious process, which was a significant finding especially in psychoanalysis. Sigmund Freud hypothesised that all humans are born innately bisexual and that homosexual people become gay because of their conditioning. But though Freud emphasised that homosexuality wasn't a disease, per se, some of his colleagues didn't agree. They began to use new psychiatric and physical interventions to 'cure' gay people.

While this started with the newly defined method of hypnosis, it soon spread to include both medical and surgical interventions as well. Some LGBTQ people were given electroconvulsive therapy, but others were subjected to even more extreme techniques like lobotomies. Other 'treatments' included shocks administered through electrodes that were implanted directly into the brain. Robert Galbraith Heath, a psychiatrist in New Orleans who pioneered this technique, used this form of brain stimulation, along with hired prostitutes and heterosexual pornography, to 'change' the sexual orientation of gay men. But though Heath claimed he was able to turn gay men straight, his work has since been challenged and criticized from a scientific viewpoint for its methodology, as well as just being generally terrible and appalling. An offshoot of these techniques was aversion therapy, which was founded on the premise that if LGBTQ people became physically disgusted by their homosexuality, they would no longer experience same-sex desire. Under medical supervision, people were given chemicals that made them vomit when they, for example, looked at photos of their lovers. Others were given electrical shocks – sometimes to their genitals – while they looked at gay pornography or cross-dressed.

Back in 1895, Schrenck-Notzing reviewed the results of his treatments with hypnosis and noted that those who achieved a deep hypnotic trance responded better. But between 1900 and 1960, there were very few studies on the use of hypnosis to 'treat' homosexuality. Peter Roper's 1967 paper documenting the successes of hypnotism in curing homosexuality theorised that this was because the process of conversion therapy was widely considered to be futile. He blamed some failures of the treatment on the fact that patients had found out that scientific consensus said that their sexuality couldn't be 'cured', and so weren't susceptible to the treatments. Another option that Roper considered for the lack of hypnotic conversion studies was his theory that psychiatrists were so disgusted by homosexuality that they couldn't even consider acknowledging it for long enough to try and treat it. There was one explanation that Roper didn't even think to consider, which was that many psychiatrists didn't think gay people needed psychological treatment.

One of the ways that investigators determined whether an individual was likely to be susceptible to conversion hypnotherapy or not, was by asking them to make a fist early in the hypnosis session. If they did, they were susceptible to the power of suggestion, and supposedly over the course of the treatment, the men's fists changed from 'homosexual fists' (with the thumb inside the fingers) to a 'masculine fist' (with the thumb on the outside.)

It would be remiss to not note as well that most conversion therapy methods have also been used to attempt to cure Disabled people, those with chronic illnesses, or those who are mentally ill. Many, like electroconvulsive therapy and lobotomies, were originally created to treat mental illnesses (or things that were assumed at the time to be mental illnesses) such as epilepsy and schizophrenia, before being adapted towards making the lives of Queer people miserable as well.

Behavioural therapy has also been used for both Queer and Disabled people (primarily Disabled children) with the aim of 'normalising' them before the age where their noticeable difference is thought to become unchangeable. The 'deviancy' or 'feeblemindedness' of these groups are seen as something to be corrected in gender non-conforming individuals as well as Autistic people. There is plenty of evidence these types of therapy are still frequently imposed on people in the present day, but there's plenty of controversy in referring to them as forms of conversion therapy. Primarily among those who perform these therapies.

Not only are they still imposed, many of the medical professionals who worked on behavioural treatments for transgender, transvestite or otherwise gender non-conforming people have since worked on extremely similar behavioural therapies for Autistic people to try and 'convert' those with noticeable autistic traits into neurotypical looking behaviours.

While many people made claims of high success rates for those undergoing treatment being able to live as heterosexual cisgender people (some claimed a 50 per cent success rate), historians, psychiatrists and Queer scholars agree that there has never been any satisfactorily documented proof that any of these methods do anything other than shame Queer people, punish Disabled people and deceive those who believe in them.

Bobbie Lea Bennet

'None of us are looking to make this thing sensational'

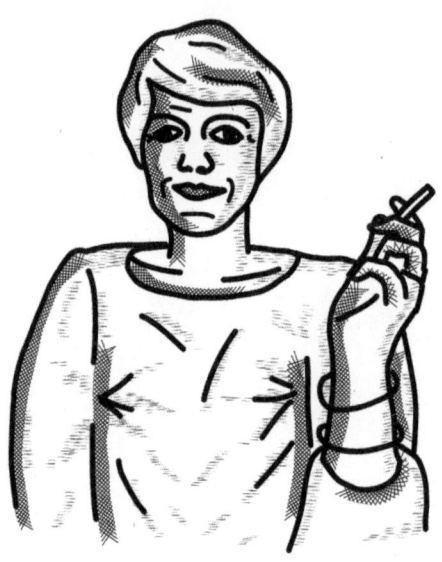

In the days prior to private health insurance, many transgender people would consider the costs of transition and having gender affirming surgery very carefully. It meant coming up with the funding for expensive treatment and rehabilitation themselves or trying to prove their gender identity and need for treatment should be considered as a disability, for the cost to be covered by social security benefits.

However, for transgender people who were disabled and on social security benefits already and paid medical costs, that step could be skipped. It was what Bobbie had originally been told.

Bobbie Lea Bennett used a wheelchair from a very young age due to a rare bone disease called osteogenesis imperfecta and spent many years during her childhood in the late 1940s and early 1950s receiving treatments. These aggressive treatments involved intense surgeries where metal rods would be screwed to her bones to strengthen them, leading to her nickname: 'bionic woman'. The doctors told her parents that she was never expected to live into adulthood, but she ignored that, refusing to acknowledge the prognosis. In her younger adult years, she worked as a dental technician, but she was consistently forced to crawl up two flights of stairs to her dental office. Since there was no lift, she was forced to pull both herself and her wheelchair up to the lab step by step every day. No-one gave it a second thought, it was just something Bobbie did to access certain places. Bobbie frequently spoke to the media and told the story of her childhood in her own words. She usually referred to her young, pre-transition self in the third person as 'he', as if the child was a different person to the vivacious and bold woman she was as an adult. Bobby told reporters that she had felt strange growing up, as if there was a disjointedness between her head and her body. It left her feeling embarrassed about the things she felt and wanted. She had always wanted to be a Brownie, not a Scout but she didn't understand why or what that meant, and it left her feeling guilty and confused. She had been raised as a Catholic, and for many years she believed she was offending God with her thoughts and feelings. Bobbie married at 18, an age that we consider young now, although this was regular at the time. She had always wanted children, and although it didn't feel right being a husband, this was the way to do it. A few years later, her wife was expecting a child, but when she was seven months pregnant she was in a car accident. She and the unborn baby died and with her, Bobbie's cherished dream of being a parent. To cope with the grief, Bobbie briefly remarried, hoping this would make her feel like a real man, and that it would allow her to fit into society's expectations. But it became clear she couldn't go on living in this way, and the marriage was annulled. She continued to feel ashamed, not understanding why she felt that way. In an interview, she described going to a women's clothing store and picking out an outfit wearing heavy make-up. When she was questioned, she told the shopkeeper it was a gift for her sister. Feeling there was something wrong with her and with no real information available to say otherwise, she went to see a psychologist in New Orleans who diagnosed her as transsexual.

This was before the first gender clinic opened in the United States, and few doctors understood gender issues at the time. Many transgenders, transsexual or cross dressing individuals thought they were sick, sinful, disgusting and perverted, and that they were alone in feeling this way. Perhaps this is why it took Bobbie five years to accept her gender identity.

While informal medical care for transgender patients had existed in an extremely informal capacity for many decades, widespread social acceptance in many communities and cultures, formally recognised gender identity clinics had a longer history than many people assume. One of the earliest and most famous, is the Institute for Sexual Science in Berlin, run by Magnus Hirschfeld. It was the first to define 'the desire to express one's gender in opposition to their defined sex' and coined the term 'transvestite'. He was one of the first to offer transition to his patients, either through hormone therapy, surgery, or both, calling it 'adaption therapy'. This facility performed surgery to construct a vagina in the early 30s, but unfortunately, most of the Institute's early work was destroyed by the Nazi regime in 1933 because of their fascism. At a similar time, Sir Harold Gillies, known by many as 'the father of plastic surgery', had been refining genital reconstruction surgical techniques on patients who had sustained wartime injuries. He found his techniques were transferable to gender affirming surgeries. He performed the first known phalloplasty on a transgender patient in the 1940s, and later started performing vaginoplasty surgeries on transgender women too. Further progress occurred across the world, with different surgeons communicating and sharing techniques to effect the best results. A surgeon in Morocco in the 1950s was credited with creating innovative new methods for vaginoplasty which improved recovery times and reduced the risk of life-threatening infections. Across the pond early gender affirming surgeries were performed in the US, including hysterectomies for trans men. This area of medicine was mostly quiet for many decades, leaving trans patients without treatment or to seek it abroad. At the same time, the University of California and John Hopkins University hospitals realised the need to perform gender affirming surgery.

Doctors working in all medical fields believed the best, and only, way to treat transgender patients was through therapy and psychoanalysis, aimed at attempting to change the person's desire to live as a different gender. The sexologist and endocrinologist Harry Benjamin is attributed with being the first physician in modern times to challenge this. In 1966, he published *The Transsexual Phenomenon*, which explained in detail the pioneering medics of the era's approach to gender affirming surgery. This book included studies of male-to-female surgical operations, such as vaginoplasty, in much more detail than female-to-male operations, such as phalloplasty or metoidioplasty. During this time, it was falsely believed that transgender men were less common than transgender women, and as a result many surgeons were more reluctant to perform gender affirming surgeries on transgender men. This has somewhat shifted in recent years, with people falsely believing that people who were assigned female at birth are much more likely to identify as a different gender and ascribe that belief to societal pressures. Based on publications from the era and anecdotal accounts, some of this reluctance stemmed from the scepticism that surgeons held, that the available surgical techniques would create a phallus that the patient would be satisfied with.

The first sparks of awareness about transgender people, and the success of gender affirming surgery, amongst both medical professionals and the American public, is credited to a woman called Christine Jorgensen. Jorgensen appeared in the New York Daily News under the headline 'Ex-GI Becomes Blonde Beauty', in an article that covered her transition and her coming out story. This captured the attention of the public and fascinated readers, as they learned about the series of operations she had undergone in Denmark between the years 1951 to 1952. This was covered in other newspapers and magazines, and Christine became a household name, and an inspiration to other transgender people – some of whom had never had a name for the way they'd been feeling.

The release of the *Transsexual Phenomenon* was quickly followed by the public announcement of the John Hopkins University Gender Identity Clinic in November 1966. While several universities thought about setting up research centres specifically to study treatments for transgender patients since the early 1960s, the opening of this clinic at John Hopkins marked a change from quiet consideration to establishing one. Initiatives became available at major universities and hospitals with different medical disciplines working together, such as psychiatrists, urologists, plastic surgeons, gynaecologists, and social workers. While no-one can agree on an exact number, the increase in US patients who underwent gender affirming surgery was dramatic, growing to more than 1,000 by the end of the 1970s from approximately 100 patients in 1969. With the advent of reputable hospitals performing this surgery it suddenly brought into reach the ability to live as your true gender.

Many of the physicians involved in the early gender identity clinics faced a lot of scepticism from colleagues. One unsympathetic colleague wrote in 1967 that 'unwittingly, many a physician does not treat the disease as such but treats rather, the fantasy a patient develops about his disease'. In the clinics' attempt to claim positive results to stave off these criticisms, they were often forced to maintain extremely rigorous selection criteria that excluded several patients in desperate need. The evaluation process required that patients undergo cross gender hormone treatment and live in the community for a set period as the gender they intended to transition to. This period could be anywhere up to five years depending on the clinic, which was a lengthy period, and caused people acute distress, especially for those who might not 'pass' as their true gender. Individuals who were considered traditionally attractive and were expected to have an easy time being a member of the other sex as individuals, who would be heterosexual when living as their accurate gender were, unfairly, considered by the clinics to be better surgical candidates. While the staff at these clinics were often the only supporters of the transgender community and advocates for their medical care, they also acted as gatekeepers. These patients would be judged by staff based on heavily enforced gender stereotypes and would often be excluded from surgeries they desperately needed for not conforming to them. The 1970s saw more gender medicine clinics close their doors to new patients. It was considered an internal decision to close certain departments of a hospital so the reason behind these closures weren't publicised and so remain unknown. We can somewhat extrapolate based on two notable exceptions to this pattern of the number of new patients quietly declining and eventually fully ceasing. The most well-known of these took place at John Hopkins University. A new chair of psychiatry, Paul McHugh was hired in 1975, who thoroughly disapproved of offering gender affirming surgery to transgender patients. He made it clear from the moment he was hired that he intended to do everything he could to stop the practice at the clinic. Under his leadership, a 1979 paper by a psychiatrist at John Hopkins University was published which cast doubts on the effectiveness of sex reassignment surgeries by suggesting that the outcomes, psychologically and socially, in transgender patients who underwent these surgeries were no better than those who didn't have surgery at all. Despite significant criticism from experienced researchers and physicians, and widely acknowledged flaws in its methodology, the study eventually led to the closure of the Johns Hopkins Gender Identity Clinic and an end to sex reassignment surgeries offered there for the transgender population. In some cases, medical care for trans patients had been taking place for many years, with no concerns, until a campaign to stop them came from beyond the medical field. This was the case at the gender identity clinic at the Baptist Medical Center in Oklahoma City. The Gender Identity Foundation had been offering a variety of services for transgender patients, including surgery, since 1973. While the medical centre was under the control of religious leaders, they seemed to have been unaware of it. In 1977, however, various issues individuals had with gender affirming surgery were brought to the board of directors of the Baptist General Convention of Oklahoma. Despite the appeals of many of the doctors on the staff who said that, '[I]f Jesus Christ were alive today, undoubtedly he would render help and comfort to the transsexual', the board of directors voted 54–2 to ban gender affirming surgery at the Baptist Medical Center. It is thought by many that the publicity around the paper that led to the closure of John Hopkins University's clinic may have played a role in the decision to close other clinics. However, it must be noted that many clinics described having financial challenges during this time, as patients were unable to afford the expensive operations due to prejudice and underemployment, and in general insurance companies refused to cover them and their sex reassignment surgeries. Even though many clinics' research began to diminish in the late 1970s, the previous fifteen years of academic interest and research motivated the 1979 establishment of the Harry Benjamin International Gender

Dysphoria Association. This organisation was formed with intentions of bringing together cross-speciality professionals who were 'interested in the study and care of transexualism and gender dysphoria'. This organisation still exists today but has since been renamed, the World Professional Association for Transgender Health (WPATH) and has now grown into an international interdisciplinary organization. The first wave of gender identity clinics allowed for a new field of medical speciality to grow, with surgical advancements and medical treatments shown to be safe and effective, despite what many people believed.

When Bobbie eventually applied for and was accepted onto a Texas hospital's gender identity programme, she knew she would live as her true self. She wanted to use her experience for good and was passionate about educating people on the issues surrounding both trans and disability rights, as well as how they intersected. Her friends said 'she was an extremely unique person and left her mark on this world, and for better. She had a strong personality; determined, extremely friendly and very sensitive'. She was also a gifted storyteller and mastered how to use the press and the publicity to her advantage. She let her warmth and love of family shine through and usually used humour to get her point across as it endeared her to people. She gained new fans and supporters by telling a reporter that she celebrated getting onto the Texas gender identity programme by treating herself to fifty new pairs of earrings, of all sizes and colours, to go with every outfit.

To qualify for the sex reassignment surgery she needed, the Gender Identity Clinic in Galveston, Texas required Bennett to live as a woman for four years before they could determine her suitability as a candidate for surgery.

Despite this obvious need for someone to openly live their true gender, and the sheer body of evidence that this treatment was necessary for individuals, there was resistance to the idea of giving them any kind of civil rights protections. During the negotiations in the American House of Senators on the Fair Housing Act in 1988, the aim of which was to prevent housing discrimination based on Disability status, a conservative senator successfully argued that people with transgender related mental illnesses, as they were considered at the time based on their inclusion in the *Diagnostic and Statistical Manual of Mental Disorders*, should be excluded from this bill. These 'transgender related mental illnesses' were referred to as transvestitism, transsexualism and gender identity disorder. This same exemption for transgender people from disability discrimination laws was adopted into the Americans with Disabilities Acts, much to the concern of Queer and Disabled activists who felt that excluding anyone from anti-discrimination legislation was both a bad idea and a slippery slope. The 1980 addition of 'gender identity disorder' to the American Psychiatric Association's third *Diagnostic and Statistical Manual* seemed like a leap backwards, but strangely, even at the time, controversial decisions may have helped transgender people gain further access to a healthcare system that was usually too complicated to enter. Thanks to tireless campaigning and lobbying from Queer activists, progress was made towards removing the language of 'disorder' in the context of gender identity, and therefore the implication that being trans was a disorder. When the 5th DSM was published in 2013, 'gender identity disorder' had been entirely replaced with the new diagnosis of 'gender dysphoria' – specifically, the distress associated with someone's assigned gender not matching their true gender.

The exclusion of 'transgender related conditions' from the ground-breaking anti-discrimination legislation, the Americans with Disabilities Act was challenged in several court cases for its unfairness in picking and choosing what conditions, illnesses and impairments it would cover. The most notable was in a case called *Blatt vs Cabela's Retail Inc.* When a woman sued the shop she worked at for firing her after revealing she was transgender and the employers tried to dismiss the case based on the ADA's transgender exclusion, the employee argued that the exclusion of transgender related conditions violated equal protection laws. She said that legally, the exclusion had to be subjected to an extra amount of scrutiny which it hadn't been, because transgender people were, and still are, a highly discriminated against minority. She argued there was no reason to exclude them other than 'a moral animus against a disfavoured group'. The court noted her points and agreed that there was a legal basis for heightened scrutiny for this clause, but in this case the court eventually concluded that 'gender identity disorder' as described in the Americans with Disabilities Act referred to transgender identity, rather than to any medical conditions a transgender person might have, such as gender dysphoria. As such, they concluded that the ADA did not protect those with a transgender identity but did cover those with the specific medical diagnosis of gender dysphoria. At this time there were no legal protections for transgender people, and being able to use the ADA to prosecute discrimination became vital for the community, even though it was not ideal they had to claim a disability status. It was still better than nothing, and so these discrimination cases trickled through the courts.

At the time that Bobbie was seeking surgery, patients would have had to undergo extensive psychological counselling and screening and it would have been necessary to present normative for that time. When a clinic approved transgender people for affirming surgery, it was on the assumption that those candidates would affirm the traditional understandings, expectations and performances of stereotypical masculinity and femininity in their post-operative life. By the mid-70s, Bobbie had been living in San Diego, California, as a woman for many years. She had finally been approved for sex reassignment surgery by her gender identity clinic, and while the surgery itself would only cost around $5,600, there would be thousands more needed for the various tests, therapies and medical care needed before and after the operation.

The American health insurance system can be difficult for many people from outside the US to understand. To prevent bankruptcy from a single illness or hospital stay, most Americans need a form of health insurance. As with any insurance, if the risk is higher, the premium paid monthly to keep the insurance, becomes higher and higher. As a result, before Medicare was created, 40 per cent of all people over 65 had no health insurance at all. This meant that any time they needed medical treatment, they would be expected to pay thousands of dollars straight from their own bank accounts. Medicare is a health insurance programme which was originally designed purely for people over the age of 65, but later extended to younger people with severe disabilities or incurable diseases. However, while they have very similar names, it is different to Medicaid, the health insurance programme for low-income households introduced by Barack Obama – often called 'Obamacare'. Introducing Medicare was an extremely long process. Congress held its first hearings on the idea of government health insurance in 1916. During the New Deal, creating widespread health coverage became a major part of the negotiations of the wider Social Security programme, but President Franklin Roosevelt decided it would be better, and easier, to pass the old-age pensions first and consider healthcare later. In 1939 Senator Robert Wagner reintroduced the idea of national health legislation to help with medical expenses for normal people and even held a few hearings to build support for it, but the world went to war. It was not until after the Second World War, in November 1945, that Harry Truman sent Congress an official proposal for the first comprehensive federal health insurance, but no-one paid any attention and nothing happened with it. This trend continued for a very long time. Despite President John F. Kennedy making Medicare a legislative priority in 1961, there was a lot of opposition from people who disapproved of government interference in healthcare, and it repeatedly stalled, until finally, in Lyndon Johnson's presidency, things started to happen. After years of attempts, on 30 July 1965, Johnson travelled to the Truman Library in Independence, Missouri, to sign Medicare into law. In recognition of his early support for a similar programme, President Truman and his wife were also invited to the event and became the first recipients of the programme.

Back in California, Bobbie Bennett had been told that the cost of her surgical procedures would be covered by Medicare and the disability benefits programme of Social Security as they covered the costs of all her medical treatment. Since they had provided payments to cover everything else, she booked her operation. However, she was told that Medicare had changed their mind about paying the cost, and decided they weren't going to fund it anymore. This isn't, and wasn't, unusual for Medicare. She was a savvy woman, an involved member of the trans community and well read on the subject. She would have known that everybody would find the approval for her surgery to be extraordinary at the time. In the run up to Bobbie's surgery, several test cases made their way to Court about gender confirmation surgery being offered on Medicare. Most of the arguments surrounded the question of whether gender confirmation surgery was medically necessary for the sake of people's health or whether it should be considered purely cosmetic. The Medicare offices had been flooded by calls and letters from 'irate taxpayers' opposing funding for sex reassignment surgery, and in response to this outpouring of hate, the Director of the Medicare Bureau said that they had received advice 'several years ago from our medical consultants that transsexual surgery was neither proven by medical evidence to be a safe and effective procedure nor accepted as such by the medical community'. However, he made it clear that while 'it was regarded as an experimental procedure… since that time, there has been increasing clinical evidence about transsexual surgery, and the Public Health Service has advised us informally that the evidence indicates the procedure can no longer be considered solely "experimental."' Despite this, gender affirming surgery was excluded from being funded by Medicare across the country, a situation that was only rectified in 2014.

But Bobbie's impairment made this all very interesting. It turned out that she was the perfect candidate to test the possibility of Medicare covering gender affirming surgery, as she could skip over the argument that many other people had to attempt to form; namely that their 'transexualism' was a form of a disability. Due to her existing impairment, all her other expenses for medical care were already covered by Medicare. That meant the only thing for the courts to consider was whether this specific surgery constituted a legitimate medical treatment. A historian focussing on this area of history, Nicholas Matte wrote that, 'her case forced Medicare to consider only one issue: whether or not Medicare would consider sex reassignment surgery a legitimate medical treatment, separate from whether otherwise healthy transsexuals would be considered disabled simply by virtue of being transsexual'. He believed that 'these controversial questions engaged not only transsexuals but also health insurers, government administrators, and sometimes the broader American public, as they involved public spending of taxpayers' money'.

The public's interest in the protection and rights of Disabled people had recently increased due to revelations in the media of the abuse and neglect of young Disabled people hidden out of sight at Willowbrook State School in New York. Bennett was able to mobilise this media interest and generate public outrage on her behalf, to have her rights respected. Willowbrook State School has a reputation which lasted long after the dissolution of the institution itself. Supported by the state and funded by the government, this care facility for children with intellectual disabilities opened in 1947 until it was closed in 1987. Staten Island, the site for the school had been used by the military during the war, and after it was no longer needed, many thought it should be used to support the disabled veterans returned from war. However, New York Governor Thomas Dewey, decided to transform it into a care facility for Disabled young people. He said that there were thousands of children who were 'mentally and physically defective and feeble minded, who never can become members of society'. Soon enough, rumours of both the conditions of the institution, the questionable medical practices and experiments they forced on the children, prompted visits from politicians to see for themselves. Senator Robert F. Kennedy told the public after one of these trips that, 'I've visited the state institutions for the mentally retarded, and I think particularly at Willowbrook, we have a situation that borders on a snake pit'. This however wasn't enough to prompt an investigation. By 1955, just eight years after it had opened, it reached its full capacity of 4,000 occupants. Around that time, reports said that hepatitis infections were rampant among patients and staff with no attempts at mitigation. Only a short time later in 1960, an outbreak of measles killed 60 patients within weeks. Far from being seen as a cause for concern, the children's rapid infection with preventable diseases on arrival at the facility was considered an opportunity by some scientists. Without the consent of either them or their parents, for fifteen years scientists quietly carried out experiments on the patients by deliberately injecting them with hepatitis. Their intention was to research and test inoculations and reasoned it was 'justifiable to inoculate retarded children at Willowbrook with hepatitis virus because most of them would get hepatitis anyway'. It wasn't until seven years after Senator Kennedy's speech that someone finally investigated the institution further. A local journalist was tipped off by a soon-to-be laid off employee, and they decided the only way to see the truth was to sneak in a journalist undercover as a new staff member, claiming they were a newly qualified social worker. The reports and images shocked the country. Many of the children had not been toilet trained, were filthy, had no clothes and weren't allowed outside. There were also several young people who clearly had physical rather than intellectual disabilities but had been misdiagnosed in childhood, meaning that it would never have been an appropriate facility for them. These young people were able to communicate, and therefore give their true accounts of the abuse and neglect. One said that 'I got beaten with sticks, belt buckles. I got my head kicked into the wall by staff', 'There was a lot of sexual abuse going on from staff to residents, also'. Finding out about this for the first time, the residents of Staten Island were outraged, and filed a class action lawsuit against both the state and the school in 1972. The success of this legal action gave way to New York State's 1975 consent decree, legally forcing the state to find alternative accommodation for the institutionalised children.

While this was far from the only incident of institutional neglect in the US, it grabbed the attention of the American people and effected a conversation about how Disabled people had been hidden from view and ignored by both the public and government. Unfortunately, stories like this are not unusual and we regularly see them crop up across the world showing how far we still must go to achieve appropriate care facilities for Disabled people. Bobbie used this outrage the American public felt to push against the infantilisation of Disabled people and the idea that they were a group who couldn't express what they wanted. She formulated an idea to force Medicare to make a decision about her surgery, ideally in her favour. She called to tell *Transition Magazine* of her plans, and after rallying the community, Bennett set off on a cross-country trip, driving from her home in San Diego to the White House in Washington, DC to promote her case, and raise awareness and garner support for her quest for appropriate healthcare. Bennett always said that there was no excuse for any woman not to look her best, she had been very strict with herself to only bring three suitcases worth of clothes on the road trip, leaving most of her giant wardrobe full of clothes and accessories at home. With her friends and family behind her and supporting her plan, she used the journey to change more hearts and minds. The journey took thirty-nine hours, and even though the hand controls in her car caused her a lot of pain, she kept herself occupied by talking to truckers on the CB radio in her car. She was incredibly popular on the airwaves and being a woman talking to truckers, some tried chatting her up. Eventually, she arrived at the White House, and was not let in. They suggested she phone instead. But unsurprisingly, six phone calls later, she was no farther in the door. She knew that it would be unlikely she would get in, but what could be considered bigger and more visible than driving to the house of the President of the United States? When it became clear that she was going to make no progress at the White House, she drove to the Baltimore office of the Social Security Headquarters and to the office of the director of Medicare. Her intention was to arrive at the office and refuse to leave until he agreed to meet with her. However, once she turned up, it was much easier than that. 'I'm Bobbie Lea Bennett' she told the receptionist and drew a wide-eyed 'oh!' in response. She was promptly ushered in to see Medicare director, Thomas M. Tierney. Looking at his huge, plush office, Bobbie exclaimed, 'so this is where my taxes go!' Tierney told her that the public doesn't realise the rigorous screening transexuals must undergo to qualify for sex-change surgery. It was said that at the time 'people [thought] that anyone [could] simply walk into a hospital and get the operation on request at the taxpayers' expense'. In their meeting, the director assured Bobbie that a specialist committee was working on the issue of gender reassignment and her case specifically, and that she would hear back from him soon about whether they would approve her for surgery or not.

Three days after Bobbie's meeting with the director of Medicare, Bobbie received a mysterious cheque in the post. The cheque happened to cover the entire cost of the surgery that they had previously refused to cover. The Medicare office claimed that they were correcting a bureaucratic error of payments owed. A few months later in April 1978, in news that was completely unrelated, the director announced a new policy that meant Medicare coverage would now be extended to gender affirming surgery, as long as the candidate had 'at least one year's experience living as a member of the opposite sex', lowered from the previous social transition requirement of 4 years. This was reported in the *New York Times* as a victory for Bobbie, where they wrote (using the wrong title and pronouns) that 'After three years of hormonal treatment and psychotherapy, which Medicare paid for, Mr. Bennett said he was told on March 23 that the program would not pay for the operation. That was reversed by yesterday's decision'. They wrote as well that this 'new policy extended Medicare coverage to sexual reassignment as long as the surgical candidates 'have at least one year's experience living as a member of the opposite sex'. Bobbie finally had her surgery in August 1978, and just a few months later Bobbie, over her CB radio, the source of much of her support and many of her romantic powers, met an electrician called Stuart Montgomery. The couple married a week later. In 1981, she and her husband went on to have a son together. Her sister acted as the surrogate and their story made it into the American news, according to a news clipping from the *Seattle Daily Times* in January 1981. The doctor who delivered the baby described Bobbie as 'a very sound, realistic sort of person' which I'm sure is how we all hope to be described someday. He added to the newspapers, I like to imagine quite sternly, that 'none of us are looking to make this thing sensational', 'Mrs. Bennett has survived a lot of things, [sex reassignment] surgery, getting married and now being prepared to raise a baby'. Bobbie said at the time that, 'We plan on having a whole bunch of babies', Mrs. Bennett said, 'Children are what make a home. I love children, and we plan on having more. We want five, three of them handicapped'. This was an incredible statement, as the idea of wanting to have a Disabled child was still completely alien to most people. She never had more than one child, but her son was a great joy in her life. A friend said that her son was 'just an awesome guy and she lived for him. Absolutely would do anything for him'. She turned her hand to many kinds of campaigning and worked for several organisations in New Orleans and Texas. The nickname 'Barbie" came about later in her life, as she was a collector and a big fan of Barbie dolls and loved the colour pink. Her friends said that 'she used to have a pink car that looked like a Barbie car but had to sell it because she started not being able to get in and out of it'. She was so well known that she had her own talk show on Texas Community Television called 'Barbie's Talk Show'. She was lucky enough to enjoy the support of her family throughout her life, and one of her favourite ways to spend an evening was playing cards with her sister, right up until she died in 2019.

At the time, Bobbie took a risk sharing her personal medical business, but her willingness to risk any outcry from the public in order to prove that her treatment was necessary, prevented thousands of others having to do the same.

Michelangelo

'Weep, you girls, my penis has given you up'

The name Michelangelo is as synonymous with Italy as the Leaning Tower of Pisa. Michelangelo di Lodovico Buonarroti Simoni is best known for his work on the Sistine Chapel and the statue of David; he is also the most documented artist of the sixteenth century.

He was born to a family that for several generations belonged to minor nobility in Florence but had, by the time the artist was born, fallen from grace and lost its status. His father held occasional government work; despite the family being down on their luck, when Michelangelo was born, they were living in the small dependent town of Caprese, where his father worked as a temporary administrator. When he was a few months old, the family returned to their home in Florence. He was a young boy when he was sent to live with a stonecutter's family as his mother became ill and was unable to care for him. When he was just six years old, she died of a long-term illness. He spoke of the family he lived with during this period of his life as having given him an innate appreciation for bashing at stones to create sculptures which later defines his life and career. 'Along with the milk of my nurse, I received the knack of handling chisel and hammer, with which I make my figures'. It was seen by many as something of a downward social step for the son of a noble to become an artist, and as a result Michelangelo became an apprentice relatively late compared with most of his peers. He was 13 years old; an old man set in his ways. Scholars ponder on whether he had to overcome objections from his father or other family members before he was allowed to pursue his dream, but he was eventually apprenticed to the city's most prominent painter, Domenico Ghirlandaio, for a three-year term. Even though such an opportunity would have been hard fought and laudable, he left that apprenticeship after one year, claiming that he had nothing more that he could learn from the artist and was done with all that.

Florence was considered a leading centre of art and culture, producing the best painters and sculptors in the whole of Europe, and to Michelangelo and his peers the competition among all the artists was stimulating and invigorating. The powerful rulers of the city had tried to surround themselves with the greatest intellectuals and artists, spurring them all on, to inspire them to create greater and greater works. The city was, however, less able to offer large commissions than they had been previously, and leading Florentine-born artists such as Leonardo da Vinci had moved on to other cities for better opportunities and more chances for funding larger projects. Michelangelo discovered marble sculpture early, after first trying sculpting in bronze and deciding he disliked it. His two most famous sculptures, David, and Pieta, were both completed before he turned thirty. The David was commissioned in 1501. Such a massive statue would have been a big and expensive commission in that city. Michelangelo created it using a block of marble which had originally been used for another project that had been left unfinished for forty years. While the sculpture was intended to be put on the buttress of the cathedral, Michelangelo convinced his peers they should place it in a more prominent place. They decided to create a commission formed of artists and prominent citizens. It was displayed in the entryway of the Palazzo dei Priori, where a replica remains to this day.

Even at this stage, Michelangelo had issues with his hands. Painful fingers and joints made sculpting both exhausting and arduous, which were themes that were reflected so significantly in his work that more recent reflections have called him 'a drama queen'. Modern experts are torn between whether he might have had gout or whether it was more likely to be another form of arthritis that we would be more familiar with now, or in fact maybe it was both, but it profoundly affected the mobility and movement of the joints in both his hands and feet for many years. According to letters he wrote to friends and loved ones, the pain was attributed to gout at the time, an ailment that caused an excess of uric acid in all the wrong places. Due to his accompanying intermittent kidney stones and a propensity in this time to refer to any inflamed 'jointy' thing as gout means that it was assumed for a long time that gout had caused him so much pain for many years. Modern interpretations have studied his portraits (the best form of medical examination, as we all know, that's why they teach it in hospitals) and found a lack of the visible signs that are usually associated with gout, making several experts believe it was more likely that he had another form of arthritis instead. Of course, we will never know for sure, and researchers from Harvard Medical School have in recent times copped out on the question entirely and suggested that he may well have had both impairments at the same time. It was partly due to this chronic pain in his hands that he continued painting alongside his sculpture, even though he was very clear with everybody he spoke to about how much he hated painting.

In 1504 he agreed to paint a huge fresco for the Sala del Gran Consiglio of the Florence City Hall. It would blend with another, just begun by Leonardo da Vinci to form a pair that was recording military victories by the city's armies. Leonardo's design shows galloping horses, while Michelangelo's is primarily of nude soldiers climbing out of a river to answer an alarm call. Alas, both works survive only in copies and parts of planning sketches. He had a habit of taking on several incredibly vast projects at a time and refusing to hire any assistants. He didn't like working with other people at all and didn't trust other artists to be able to help complete his work. This meant that most of the major projects he started in his life remained unfinished. One might find this surprising considering his reputation.

He was commissioned in 1505 to create a set of twelve marble Apostles for the Florence cathedral, which he did begin working on, but the progress was slow. Some have said that the figures that he did start almost look like they're struggling to remove themselves. Maybe this would make you think that it was deliberate that they remained unfinished, like he was making an artistic statement. However, it's much more likely that he really wanted to finish them all but just never got round to it. Instead of finishing the sculptures he wrote a sonnet about how hard it was for the artist to draw the perfect figure out from the stone, so it's clear that he was irritated by this inability to complete the tasks.

Michelangelo had been staunchly Catholic from childhood; so Catholic in fact that he allegedly had an affair with the pope. Or at least that's what some people say. Most experts think that the chances of any kind of sexual relationship between Michelangelo and Pope Julius II is incredibly unlikely (even though this particular pope did have a child, in stark contrast to the vow of celibacy that we associate popes with today). Similarly, by this point Michelangelo was an older man, and so although homoerotic sexual relationships were relatively commonplace, even for otherwise heterosexual men, these were nearly exclusively with young men and boys.

Later in that same year, Michelangelo was summoned to Rome by the newly elected Pope Julius. Forced to leave Florence and yet another unfinished work, this time a painting of the Battle of Cascina, he was commissioned to build a special new tomb for the pope. It was planned to be very complex and ornate, including forty separate statues and even with this level of complication, it was due to be finished in five years. This was probably sensible, considering how old popes normally are when they're elected. Since he was sponsored by the pope, Michelangelo was constantly interrupted from his work on the tomb to complete any other little artistic tasks that the pope came up with.

This infuriated our maestro and the two of them would have constant rows due to their strong personalities. Julius was clearly concerned by how much all his projects were costing him, and he would pull the artist away from his work on the tomb, putting Michelangelo onto much cheaper and quicker projects, that were more likely to give him a return on his investment. Michelangelo returned to Florence until the pope became so annoyed that he pressured the city authorities enough that they were forced to send him back to Rome to finish all of his art jobs.

After he was dragged back, he agreed to do another job as a personal favour to the pope, which may seem weird considering how much they fought, but Michelangelo was still a Catholic, after all. This job was a commission to paint some frescoes on the ceiling of a church in the Vatican called the Sistine Chapel. Although he saw painting as the lesser of the arts, he agreed, since who can say no to the pope.

However, according to the account of Condivi, a 'mediocre' but fellow artist and biographer of Michelangelo, there was an ulterior motive for this commission. Another sculptor, Bramante, who was working on St. Peter's Basilica, hated Michelangelo, and resented him for being given the commission for the pope's tomb. Hoping for some drama, he convinced the pope to commission Michelangelo again, but this time in his less practised art style. He hoped that the sculptor would fail and be cast aside from the retinue of successful artists in the pope's employ.

However, his plan was unsuccessful. Michelangelo was originally commissioned to paint the Twelve Apostles on the otherwise quite plain and seemingly irrelevant ceiling. Ceilings normally showed only individual figures, rather than dramatic scenes so it originally wasn't expected to be a big job. However, over the course of four years (which included a short break when he wasn't paid and so refused to do any painting), Michelangelo persuaded Pope Julius II to give him the freedom to be bolder and proposed a much more complicated and unusual series of figures and scenes. He painted the figures of the seven prophets and five sibyls (the name for female prophets) around the edges of the ceiling and filled all the vast empty space inside that outline with scenes from Genesis. He included scenes depicting the Creation of the World, the stories of Adam and Eve, the life of Noah and the 40 generations of Jesus Christ's ancestry that were referenced in the genealogy section of the Bible.

Michelangelo had to paint all 12,000 square feet of the Sistine Chapel while lying on a scaffolding system he made himself with his legs dangling off the end. There was no support for his neck as he needed to be within a few inches of the ceiling itself with his arm outstretched to get the level of detail he needed, and this left him in agonising pain. The artist Vasari reported that he had to 'work with his face looking upwards, which impaired his sight so badly that he could not read or look at drawings, save with his head turned backwards... for several months afterwards'. Because Visari had seen this, and how much pain he himself had been in when he painted a much smaller series of ceilings, he was 'astonished that Michelangelo bore all that discomfort so well'.

The sheer size and scale of the project took a toll on his body. In a letter he wrote to Giovanni da Pistoia, he included a tragic (or, depending on how you look at it, very funny) poem describing his physical pain. This included his complaints that: 'my brain's crushed in a casket [and] my breast twists like a harpy's' and moaning that 'my haunches are grinding into my guts [and] my poor ass strains to work as a counterweight'.

But although Disability in poetry doesn't have a particularly extensive history, Michelangelo is far from the only person to write of his ailments or impairments, and to consider how the Disabled experience interacts with creative writing.

John Kitto was primarily a Biblical scholar and writer from Devon although online sources point out he had Cornish ancestry. Living in the nineteenth century in a poor family, he spent some of his childhood in a workhouse, being used as cheap labour instead of going to school. While working and living in this place, he fell from a tall ladder and landed on his head. He became permanently Deaf and never grew another inch in height for the rest of his life. Throughout his teenage years, and right into his adulthood, he underwent many treatments for his Deafness (at this time, 'curing Deafness' was actually a priority for medical scientists) but eventually he decided that he wasn't interested in trying to find any kind of treatment or cure, as 'the condition in which two-thirds of my life has been passed, has become a habit to me – a part of my physical nature'. He was grateful for his accident and his Deafness, as it had given him both the time and the desire to read all sorts of books on a wider range of subjects than many of his peers, and thus significantly broadened his horizons. While most of his work was religious in nature, he was eventually convinced by curious people to write a vaguely autobiographical study on the loss of his hearing. In the book, which he called *The Lost Senses*, he wrote that it was impossible for Deaf people to write poetry, as they do not and cannot 'have that knowledge of quantity and rhyme which is essential to harmonious verse'. However, he then followed this up with his own attempt at 'the tuneful art', showing that it wasn't very impossible at all. His newfound confidence in his Deaf identity however clearly battled with his feelings of inadequacy from his lack of hearing: how else could someone veer so quickly between writing original poetry and denying someone like him could ever do such a thing?

Feelings of inadequacy rising from a disability or impairment is unfortunately still commonplace today. It is seen by many as an unavoidable stage of acceptance of one's Disabled identity. On the plus side, it has created a whole extra layer of inspiration for artists, and many have explored it in their visual art, creative writing, and poetry. However, no matter how much work anyone does to prove Disabled people are just the same, and just as capable, as everyone else, it doesn't stop people from feeling like they're irreparably broken when they become impaired.

This was a major ongoing theme in Wilfred Owen's wartime poetry, particularly one named Disabled. An anti-war poem told from the perspective of a wounded soldier, it speaks of how the rest of this young man's life will likely be, now he has lost both of his legs and, boy, is it grim. The patient is 'sat in a wheeled chair, waiting for dark', and reflects on his war time experience. He remembers that back when he first returned from the front, no-one seemed pleased to see him or celebrated him being home. 'Only a solemn man who brought him fruits, thanked him; and then inquired about his soul'. In this situation, the soldier would be forced to simply 'spend a few sick years in institutes, and do what things the rules consider wise, and take whatever pity they may dole'. The frustration and anger of how these soldiers would be treated by society is palpable from the writing, but the framing of this poem implying that the fear of becoming Disabled is enough to end the concept of war is one that could make many Disabled people in the modern day stop and think to themselves 'hang on a minute, it's not that bad!' For Wilfred Owen, who dealt with shellshock during his time in the trenches, using these kind of shock tactics is not too surprising given the horrors of war that he was experiencing every day during the First World War. He is more recently thought by many who have studied his work to have been gay due to the extremely graphic, homoerotic themes in some of his poetry.

In the last few decades, poetry by Disabled people has been becoming more and more popular. Through creative writing, Disabled people can change assumptions about Disability and impairment and challenge stereotypes. Many Disabled artists say that they also use it as an outlet to process and cope with the pain or discomfort associated with their impairments (as Michelangelo could've done with) and the mental stress of living in a world not designed for Disability.

Michelangelo's high-profile projects, buddying up with the pope and repainting the fresco meant that, unlike most tortured artists we're familiar with, he was appreciated in his own time. He is known to be the first western artist to have a biography of his life published before he even died. Not only once, but twice, in two rival books. In an age where every minor celebrity writes an autobiography in time for Christmas this may not sound that unusual, but in that era, a biography being published while the subject was still alive and continuing to do things was a very strange thing, essentially a story with no ending. The first one of these was the end chapter in a book chronicling artists' lives in 1550 by the painter and architect Giorgio Vasari. It was the only chapter in the entire series that profiled a living artist, and it explicitly presented Michelangelo's works as the pinnacle of art, a culmination of all artistic study that had ever existed and unsurpassed by anyone who came before him. However, Michelangelo himself wasn't all that keen on how he was portrayed in this chapter and so arranged for his assistant Ascanio Condivi to write another book in 1553. This was probably based on the artist's own dictated words, which would portray him as he wanted to, and should, appear to future generations. Once Michelangelo had died, Vasari published a second edition where he defended his characterisation and had another go, like someone shouting 'AND ANOTHER THING' long after an argument has ended. While scholars have often preferred Condivi's book as the likely more reliable source, Vasari's writing style, its historical importance, and the sheer number of times it's been reprinted in different languages have made it the more used reference for the standard ideas about not just Michelangelo, but a lot of other Renaissance artists as well.

After Pope Julius' death in 1512, the funding for his tomb was cut off. A strange decision given he needed the tomb more than ever, but I guess it's hard to calculate the budget postmortem. His elected successor was Pope Leo X, a member of the Medici family who had been a friend of Michelangelo since they were both children. He must have thought he'd won the jackpot with a pal who would give him the money and time to finish his existing projects, but alas sixteenth century Papal power dynamics meant that soon enough the new Pontiff became embroiled in an inevitable disagreement with the family of the previous pope, and their papal families became deathly enemies.

Michelangelo was completely incapable of hiding his frustration at this development. He had very little patience for anyone's nonsense at the best of times, let alone when it was based on a personal feud that made no sense to him.

Incidents, such as this and his reactions to them, have given most people the impression that he was unable to maintain any kind of relationship. This, among many other traits, has led to many people in more recent years considering whether he was Autistic. As any historian of disability will tell you, retroactively diagnosing people from history with certain impairments is fraught with issues, but this view is one shared by many so called experts (not that I've studied their credentials), so who am I to say it's not true? Of course, most people would tell you that to base this entirely on his somewhat brusque personality would be inadequate. A paper in 2004 based their pseudo diagnosis on his reported 'single-minded work routine, unusual lifestyle, limited interests, poor social and communication skills, and issues of life control' which is not only a misunderstanding of neurodivergent traits, but also insulting to Autistic people. This 'unusual lifestyle' primarily consists of several personality traits which individually wouldn't be that unusual. He was said to be very frugal, telling an apprentice that, 'however rich I may have been, I have always lived like a poor man'. This attitude probably explains how studies of all his bank accounts and assets show that his net worth was about 50,000 gold ducats, more than many princes and dukes of his time.

He was said to be apparently indifferent to food and drink, eating 'more out of necessity than of pleasure' and that he 'often slept in his clothes and ... boots'. Similarly, yet another biographer wrote that, 'His nature was so rough and uncouth that his domestic habits were incredibly squalid' which meant that he didn't take on any students to carry forth his knowledge. This was probably not a huge problem for him, as he usually 'withdrew himself from the company' of other people. Some people would describe him as solitary or melancholy. I would say he was just sick of them all. These habits worked in his favour when it came to his tasks as a commissioned artist. He would work towards his goal, ignoring other needs or wants, but would then get very annoyed when he was suddenly supposed to change directions.

Under the rule of Pope Leo X, Michelangelo began working on a more architectural style of sculpture and was put to work on what would become a new attachment to the Medici chapel. Named after the ruling family, two younger members had died, and the family wanted them to be aptly, and grandly, commemorated. Michelangelo's focus was on the inside of this chapel, with both the designs on the walls and the figures on the tombs being carved individually from marble. The four carved figures, Night, Day, Dusk and Dawn are so large, front and centre, that they are always spotted by visitors long before the effigies of the young men themselves.

During those same years, Michelangelo designed another annex to the same church, called the Laurentian Library. This was a vital and urgent addition, needed to store all the books that were donated by Pope Leo after his death. It was traditional in Florence and elsewhere that libraries were housed in convents and other religious places, but alas our artist was restricted by the existing building. However, Michelangelo's knowledge of architecture would soon come in very handy when the city of Rome was besieged.

Charles V, the Holy Roman Emperor, never actually meant to storm the city. It just sort of happened. While the names sound similar and originated from the same area, the Papal States (a good chunk of Italy including Rome) and the Holy Roman Empire (an early German political empire) were officially independent of each other after the Treaty of Venice in 1177. Charles just wanted to be a bit threatening, but before he knew it, his unpaid and 'mutinous' troops had stormed in, looting and slaying the citizens of the barely defended city. The pope ran off, and the city overthrew their Medici rulers, for a couple of years at least, until in 1530 they in turn besieged the whole place and returned to rule the city forever and ever. There was more to this event than just what I've mentioned here, but Michelangelo didn't really care about all that. He was much more attached to the city rather than any system of government. However, during the siege, he was the designer of some of the major fortifications. He defended areas by designing structures which were resistant to cannon fire, as well as normal fighting, and that could be speedily built from things that were already lying around. Many of the surviving drawings of these plans have been admired for their skill and ingenuity.

In 1534 Michelangelo left Florence for the last time, though he always hoped to be able to return to finish all the projects that he had left incomplete. He returned to Rome, and as he continued to age, he became increasingly anxious about his health and his inevitable death. The progression of his creativity into the form of his poetry was partly due to the further deterioration in his joints and the additional pain these were now causing him. The amount that he was writing drastically increased and today we have around three hundred preserved poems. These included about seventy-five finished sonnets and about ninety-five finished madrigals (which were a form of poetry like a sonnet, but generally freer and looser with fewer rules). Many of his poems were addressed to young men that he became infatuated with. In fact, most of them are to one man. While many people would consider love poetry from one man to another as a clear sign of homosexuality, many people still deny that he was Queer, with some claiming that 'his sexual orientation cannot be confirmed, as no similar indications had emerged when the artist was younger'. Naturally some are so reluctant to consider his potential non-heterosexuality that they even claim that his long lasting (as far as I can tell, completely platonic) friendship with a widow called Vittoria was the inspiration for much of his poetry, even though it was addressed to specific men by name and used specifically male pronouns. The longest sequence of verse, displaying deep romantic feeling, was written to Tommaso dei Cavalieri, who was 23 years old when Michelangelo first met him as a much older man. He was described later as an 'incomparable beauty', with 'graceful manners, so excellent an endowment and so charming a demeanour that he indeed deserved, and still deserves, the more to be loved the better he is known'. The series of poems he wrote to Tommaso remain to this day to be the first known love poems written by one man to another in modern language. Cavalieri replied: 'I swear to return your love. Never have I loved a man more than I love you, never have I wished for a friendship more than I wish for yours'. Very not gay. Cavalieri remained devoted to Michelangelo until his death. Many experts believe that their relationship was chaste, but there were almost undoubtedly other sexual relationships that Michelangelo had with young men. In 1542, he had met Cecchino dei Bracci who tragically died only a year later, inspiring Michelangelo to write forty-eight funeral epigrams which were quite graphic in a way that wasn't always appreciated by the young man's family. Some of the objects of Michelangelo's affections, and subjects of his poetry, were known to have taken advantage of him: the model Febo di Poggio asked for money in response to a love-poem, and a second model, Gherardo Perini, was said to have shamelessly stolen from him. Poetry about these men feature plenty of metaphors which are hard to interpret as anything other than physical expressions of sexuality. However, the male objects of many of his poems were repressed after his death. His grandnephew, on finding the poetry in 1623, published them with the gender of pronouns changed, and it was not until a new English translation in 1893 that this was eventually noticed, and all changed back. This habit of repressing someone's sexuality after they die has been relatively common with noteworthy figures from history, as well as hiding their disabilities.

While these sonnets predate much homoromantic modern language writings, in the ancient world you could barely move without falling over another homoerotic poem. Homoerotic poetry is a genre made up of poems featuring either allusions to Queerness or undeniable gay on gay action. This type of verse has been written for so long that the walls of the destroyed city of Pompeii contain graffiti by a young man in the throes of a new discovery, as he decided to carve into the stone to tell the straight women of the world to 'weep, you girls, my penis has given you up'. In many places in the ancient world, gay sexual relationships were not in any way uncommon. For many, it was considered normal, particularly for high status individuals, to have sexual relationships with very young men, in fact often boys. This quite rightly would disgust us now, often the boys involved were the same age as girls who were being married off to much older men to start having babies. Of course, I'm not defending it, just giving some context.

In ancient Greece, most poets were 'classical', writing about myths and Gods. However, one man, Callus, decided to do something a bit different and instead write about his own life. Born in 82BC, by writing his poetry he told the heartwarming tales of his Queerness and saved them for us so that we can still read them today. A lot of the poem I cannot repeat here, but I will mention that he uses the line (translated into English) 'I will butt-fuck you and skull-fuck you!'

In the Muslim state of al-Andalus in the Middle East in the eighth century, while homosexuality wasn't permitted, the sheer amount of homoerotic poetry showed it was at least tolerated in day-to-day life, even if not openly accepted. At the time, they didn't have the social constructs for the terms 'gay' and 'straight', only who the 'passive' participant was and who was the 'active' participant.

Sex with young men was a very common activity for many Kings and their staff, so much so that no-one really batted an eyelid when the classical poet Abu Nuwas wrote about the subject. In writings about his life, Abu Nuwas recounted his many sexual relationships with women and teenage boys, how he liked 'young men in military training or even those who have started growing facial hair' and wrote a poem about his love for another man which was like 'unbreakable rope'.

However much like Abu Nuwas, Michelangelo's sexuality didn't seem to be all that hidden at the time. After getting a bad response to his painting *The Last Judgement* in the Sistine Chapel, he was publicly accused of being godless and homosexual by a well-known satirist. Michelangelo responded to this accusation by adding the face of the satirist to the painting, depicting him as an unflattering figure being dragged to hell. This appeared to be one of his favourite methods for dealing with critics who he thought were overstepping their artistic opinions. He got quite a lot of criticism for one painting of the second coming of Christ, where every single figure was not only naked, but also extremely handsomely muscular. After the pope's assistant said that it was 'no work for a papal chapel but rather for the public baths and taverns', Michelangelo waited for him to leave the room, then instantly painted his face from memory into the scene as the judge of the underworld, complete with donkey ears and a coiled snake covering his groin. On complaining to the pope about his depiction, the pope said that since he didn't have any authority over the pits of hell, the painting would have to stay as it was.

Michelangelo was the head architect of St Peter's in the Vatican when he died in 1564, leaving many projects, including the Dome of St Peter, unfinished. In the end, many of his pieces were never completed, although some of them were finished by other people. Whether he would have approved of that or not, it's hard to say, but guess would be 'no'. *The Last*

Judgement, or its revisions at least, were completed by an artist called da Volterra, after a Vatican council meeting decided the genitals needed to be covered for the sake of everyone's souls. While I'm sure he was an incredibly accomplished artist in every other way, after taking on this task he became known as 'il Braghettone' or in English, 'the Breeches Maker', a name which hilariously followed him around for the rest of his life and into the modern day. There are worse things to be known for than as Michelangelo's pants painter.

Acknowledgements

The Spotted Cow
The Steam Crane
The Rising Sun
   Alpha Bottle Shop
The Ostrich
The Apple
The Llandoger Trow
The Lyon's Den
The Rose and Crown
The Kingswood Colliers
The Dark Horse
The Old Stillage
   Grounded
The Orchard
The Old Castle Green
The Old Market Tavern

Bibliography

Abse, L., 2011. *BBC – Archive – The Gay Rights Movement – Today.* Leo Abse. Retrieved from https://web.archive.org/web/20110818134241/http://www.bbc.co.uk/archive/gay_rights/12005.shtml

ADA History – In Their Own Words: Part One | ACL Administration for Community Living. Retrieved from https://acl.gov/ada/origins-of-the-ada

Alan Turing – a short biography. Retrieved from https://www.turing.org.uk/publications/dnb.html

Alan Turing – Computer Designer Codebreaker Enigma | Britannica. Retrieved from https://www.britannica.com/biography/Alan-Turing/Computer-designer

Alan Turing and the Hidden Heroes of Bletchley Park | The National WWII Museum | New Orleans. Retrieved from https://www.nationalww2museum.org/war/articles/alan-turing-betchley-park

Al-Andalus. Homoerotic Poetry. An Unexpected Discovery. Retrieved from https://www.spainthenandnow.com/spanish-literature/al-andalus-poetry-homoerotic-verse

Barbara Jordan: African American Politician (Journey to Freedom) Joseph D. McNair 2000

Barbara Jordan | Biography & Facts | Britannica. Retrieved from https://www.britannica.com/biography/Barbara-Jordan

Barbara Jordan | National Museum of African American History and Culture. Retrieved from https://nmaahc.si.edu/barbara-jordan

Barbara Jordan | Research Guides at Library of Congress. Retrieved from https://guides.loc.gov/barbara-jordan/introduction

Barbara Jordan – Hiding in Plain Sight. Retrieved from http://www.raggededgemagazine.com/extra/bjordan.htm

Barbara Jordan: a Radical Victorian. Publisher: Hassell Street Press. Webb R. K. Publication Date: 2021

BBC – Archive – The Gay Rights Movement – Today | Leo Abse. Retrieved from https://web.archive.org/web/20110818134241/http://www.bbc.co.uk/archive/gay_rights/12005.shtml

Black Woman in Texas Is Governor for a Day – The New York Times. Retrieved from https://www.nytimes.com/1972/06/11/archives/black-woman-in-texas-is-governor-for-a-day.html

Bobbie Lea Bennett | Tan France's Queer Icons | Podcasts on Audible.

Retrieved from https://www.audible.co.uk/pd/Ep-2-Bobbie-Lea-Bennett-Podcast/B095ZRYMPH

BRING SHARON HOME / D.C. LESBIAN COMMITTEE TO FREE SHARON KOWALSKI · Documented | Digital Collections of The History Project. Retrieved from https://historyproject.omeka.net/items/show/71

Byron, G. G. N. (1788–1824). poet | Oxford Dictionary of National Biography. Retrieved from https://www.oxforddnb.com/display/10.1093/ref:odnb/9780198614128.001.0001/odnb-9780198614128-e-4279;jsessionid=6F3A92CD0ECB9A4F25709AFDF677B42F#odnb-9780198614128-e-4279-div1-d3114e5803

Camping It Up in Ancient Rome: A Queer Take on Catullus 16 | HuffPost Voices. Retrieved from https://www.huffpost.com/entry/ancient-rome-homosexuality_b_2813920

Carter, D., 2004. *Stonewall: The Riots That Sparked the Gay Revolution*. Retrieved from https://www.amazon.co.uk/Stonewall-Riots-That-Sparked-Revolution/dp/0312671938

Charles, C., 2006. *Sharon Kowalski Case: Lesbian and Gay Rights on Trial*. Retrieved from https://www.booksamillion.com/p/Sharon-Kowalski-Case/Casey-Charles/9780700612666?id=8676427353025

Conversion Therapy – Part 1: Where it Comes From. Retrieved from https://coupleandfamilyclinic.com/conversion-therapy-part-1-where-it-comes-from

Dykes Disability & Stuff – Wikipedia. Retrieved from https://en.wikipedia.org/wiki/Dykes_Disability_%26_Stuff

Disability History: The Disability Rights Movement (U.S. National Park Service). Retrieved from https://www.nps.gov/articles/disabilityhistoryrightsmovement.htm

Don Leon – Google Books. Retrieved from https://www.google.co.uk/books/edition/Don_Leon/2tc6AQAAMAAJ?hl=en&gbpv=1&printsec=frontcover

Don't fall for the myth that it's 50 years since we decriminalised homosexuality | Peter Tatchell | The Guardian. Retrieved from https://www.theguardian.com/commentisfree/2017/may/23/fifty-years-gay-liberation-uk-barely-four-1967-act

Eternal Flame: Britain Europe Exotica America – Google Books. Retrieved from https://books.google.co.uk/books?id=eSvmMgEACAAJ&redir_esc=y

Ep 2: Bobbie Lea Bennett | Tan France's Queer Icons | Podcasts on

Audible. Retrieved from https://www.audible.co.uk/pd/Ep-2-Bobbie-Lea-Bennett-Podcast/B095ZRYMPH

Fryer, J. 1972. Speech of Dr Henry Anonymous (John Fryer) at the American Psychiatric Association 125th Annual Meeting 2 May 1972 | 217 Boxes of Dr Henry Anonymous. Retrieved from http://217boxes.com/speech/

Fuentes, C., 2006. *The Diary of Frida Kahlo: An Intimate Self-Portrait.* Abrams.

Gay Conversion Therapy's Disturbing 19th-Century Origins | HISTORY. Retrieved from https://www.history.com/.amp/news/gay-conversion-therapy-origins-19th-century

Gay Conversion Therapy's Disturbing 19th-Century Origins. Retrieved from https://www.history.com/.amp/news/gay-conversion-therapy-origins-19th-century

Gay Is Good: History of Homosexuality in the DSM and Modern Psychiatry | American Journal of Psychiatry Residents' Journal. Retrieved from https://ajp.psychiatryonline.org/doi/10.1176/appi.ajp-rj.2022.180103

Gayexplained.com, 2023. The Ancient Gay Graffiti of Pompeii. Retrieved from https://www.gayexplained.com/gay-graffiti-pompeii

Gordon Brown issues apology for treatment of Alan Turing. Retrieved from https://www.manchester.ac.uk/discover/news/gordon-brown-issues-apology-for-treatment-of-alan-turing/

Harriet Martineau: a Radical Victorian. Publisher: Hassell Street Press. Webb R. K. Publication Date: 2021

Herrera, H., 2002. *Frida: A Biography of Frida Kahlo.* Harper Perennial.

Historicizing Liberal American Transnormativities: Media Medicine Activism 1960-1990 | TSpace Repository. Retrieved from https://tspace.library.utoronto.ca/handle/1807/68460

How Persons with Intellectual Disabilities Are Fighting for Decision-Making Rights | Current History | University of California Press. Retrieved from https://online.ucpress.edu/currenthistory/article/121/831/30/119205/How-Persons-with-Intellectual-Disabilities-Are

How Barbara Jordan's 1974 Speech Marked a Turning Point in the Watergate Scandal | HISTORY. Retrieved from https://www.history.com/news/barbara-jordan-speech-nixon-impeachment

Hypnotism: A History Derek Forrest Penguin Books Ltd 2001

In re Peery 556 Pa. 125 | Casetext Search + Citator. Retrieved from https://casetext.com/case/in-re-peery-2

Introduction – HIV and Disability – NCBI Bookshelf. Retrieved from https://www.ncbi.nlm.nih.gov/books/NBK209952/

It's Not the 80s Anymore: Transition-Related Care is Basic Healthcare | ACLU. Retrieved from https://www.aclu.org/news/lgbtq-rights/its-not-80s-anymore-transition-related-care-basic-healthcare

Kitty Cone: Advocate for Disability Rights | Smithsonian American Women's History. Retrieved from https://womenshistory.si.edu/stories/kitty-cone-advocate-disability-rights

Letters of Note: Yours in distress Alan. Retrieved from https://web.archive.org/web/20130120024901/http://www.lettersofnote.com/2012/06/yours-in-distress-alan.html

Medical Rights for Same-Sex Couples and Rainbow Families. Retrieved from https://scholarship.richmond.edu/cgi/viewcontent.cgi?referer=&httpsredir=1&article=1044&context=law-student-publications

Medicare ban on sex reassignment surgery lifted. Retrieved from https://eu.usatoday.com/story/news/nation/2014/05/30/medicare-sex-reassignment/9789675/

MinnPost, 2018. 30 years ago, M. Sue Wilson and 'National Free Sharon Kowalski Day' helped spark the gay marriage movement in Minnesota. Retrieved from https://www.minnpost.com/community-sketchbook/2018/08/30-years-ago-m-sue-wilson-and-national-free-sharon-kowalski-day-helped/

Nicolson, J., 2019. *MP proposes new law to pardon people with historic convictions for being gay.* London Evening Standard. Retrieved from https://www.standard.co.uk/news/uk/mp-proposes-new-law-to-pardon-people-with-historic-convictions-for-being-gay-a3284366.html

No Sorrow No Pity: Intersections of Disability HIV/AIDS and Gay Male Masculinity in the 1980s | Disability Studies Quarterly. Retrieved from https://dsq-sds.org/index.php/dsq/article/view/7148/5950

Oppy, G. & Dowe, D., 2011. *The Turing Test.* Stanford Encyclopedia of Philosophy. Retrieved from https://plato.stanford.edu/entries/turing-test/

Pardon for gay men convicted under abolished laws – BBC News. Retrieved from https://www.bbc.co.uk/news/uk-scotland-50002745

Pathologizing Sexual Deviance: A History: The Journal of Sex Research: Vol 50 No 3–4. Retrieved from https://www.tandfonline.com/doi/abs/10.1080/00224499.2012.738259

Petition seeks apology for Enigma code-breaker Turing. CNN.com. Retrieved from https://edition.cnn.com/2009/WORLD/europe/09/01/alan.turing.petition/index.html

Political Organizer for Disability Rights 1970s–1990s and Strategist for Section 504 Demonstrations 1977. Retrieved from https://oac.cdlib.org/view?docId=kt1w1001mt&brand=oac4&doc.view=entire_text

Pride and Protest – LGBT+ Disability Activism 1985–1995. Retrieved from https://review.gale.com/2021/12/03/lgbt-disability-activism-in-the-us/

Queer Elders Are Going Into Care – And Back Into the Closet | Novara Media. Retrieved from https://novaramedia.com/2021/06/11/queer-elders-are-going-into-care-and-back-into-the-closet/

Queerplaces – Muhammad bin Dawud al-Zahiri. Retrieved from http://www.elisarolle.com/queerplaces/klmno/Muhammad%20bin%20Dawud%20al-Zahiri.html

Regulating sex and sexuality: the 20th century – UK Parliament. Retrieved from https://www.parliament.uk/about/living-heritage/transformingsociety/private-lives/relationships/overview/sexuality20thcentury/

Shakespeare, T., 2019. *The social model of disability: an outdated ideology?*. University of Murcia. Retrieved from https://www.um.es/discatif/PROYECTO_DISCATIF/Textos_discapacidad/00_Shakespeare2.pdf

Society for Human Rights | Legacy Project Chicago. Retrieved from https://legacyprojectchicago.org/milestone/society-human-rights#:~:text=Despite%20its%20brief%20existence%20andabout%20until%20three%20decades%20later

Stonewall 1979: The Drag of Politics – The Village Voice. Retrieved from https://www.villagevoice.com/stonewall-1979-the-drag-of-politics/

Stryker, S., 2016. "Transgender Activism" (PDF). glbtq archives. Retrieved 6 February 2016.

The 1977 Disability Rights Protest That Broke Records and Changed Laws – Atlas Obscura. Retrieved from https://www.google.com/amp/s/www.atlasobscura.com/articles/504-sit-in-san-francisco-1977-disability-rights-advocacy.amp

The Ancient Gay Graffiti of Pompeii. Retrieved from https://www.gayexplained.com/gay-graffiti-pompeii/

The Church of England Homosexual Law Reform and the Shaping of the Permissive Society 1957–1979 | Journal of British Studies

| Cambridge Core. Retrieved from https://www.cambridge.org/core/journals/journal-of-british-studies/article/church-of-england-homosexual-law-reform-and-the-shaping-of-the-permissive-society-19571979/5EC8FD816022B79F2F4B12CD7DE94CA7

The Diary of Frida Kahlo: An Intimate Self-Portrait by Carlos Fuentes 2006 Abrams

The Fields of HIV and Disability: past present and future – PMC. Retrieved from https://www.ncbi.nlm.nih.gov/pmc/articles/PMC2788341/

The Long History of Same-Sex Marriage – JSTOR Daily. Retrieved from https://daily.jstor.org/the-long-history-of-same-sex-marriage/

The Loves of Frida Kahlo: Mexico's Most Famous Bisexual. Retrieved from https://www.thepinknews.com/2023/07/06/frida-kahlo-birthday-bisexual-artist/

The Man Who Made the UK Say "I'm Sorry For What We Did To Turing." | WIRED. Retrieved from https://www.wired.com/2014/11/the-man-who-made-the-uk-say-im-sorry-for-what-we-did-to-turing/

The Minnesota legal fight that changed the course of the gay rights movement – Minnesota Lawyer. Retrieved from https://minnlawyer.com/2018/08/03/the-minnesota-legal-fight-that-changed-the-course-of-the-gay-rights-movement/

The Passions of Michelangelo. Retrieved from https://rictornorton.co.uk/michela.htm

The Psychology of Human Sexuality – Justin J. Lehmiller – Google Books. Retrieved from https://books.google.co.uk/books?id=JXJGDwAAQBAJ&redir_esc=y

The State of Transgender Health Care: Policy Law and Medical Frameworks – PMC. Retrieved from https://www.ncbi.nlm.nih.gov/pmc/articles/PMC3953767/

The Wolfenden Report 1957 conclusion | The British Library. Retrieved from https://www.bl.uk/collection-items/wolfenden-report-conclusion

Tough Texas Women Chapter One: Barbara Jordan. Retrieved from https://www.austintexas.gov/sites/default/files/files/Parks/Dickinson/TTW_-_Barbara_Jordan_EDIT.pdf

Turing Alan Mathison (1912–1954) mathematician and computer scientist | Oxford Dictionary of National Biography. Retrieved from https://www.oxforddnb.com/display/10.1093/ref:odnb/9780198614128.001.0001/odnb-9780198614128-e-36578?rskey=Fk5NFs&result=2

Uncovering the History of Guardianship – YouTube. Retrieved from https://www.youtube.com/watch?v=0yx2dAKfeuw

Why Did the Mafia Own the Bar? | American Experience | Official Site | PBS. Retrieved from https://www.pbs.org/wgbh/americanexperience/features/stonewall-why-did-mafia-own-bar/

Willowbrook the institution that shocked a nation into changing its laws | by Matt Reimann | Timeline. Retrieved from https://timeline.com/willowbrook-the-institution-that-shocked-a-nation-into-changing-its-laws-c847acb44e0d

Index

504 Sit-In 51-54, 150
Accessibility (Activism) 18, 41, 45, 60-62, 70-71, 193
Accessibility (Law) 50, 56, 73-74
Accessible Toilets 68-69
Accessible Transport 56, 60-62
AIDS Coalition to Unleash Power 33-38
AIDS Quilt 38
Alan Turing 115, **117**-129, 133
Albert von Schrenck-Notzig 187-189
Alf Morris 19
Americans Disabled for Accessible Public Transit (ADAPT) 60-62
American Disabled for Attendant Programs Today (ADAPT) 95
American Federation of the Physically Handicapped 149
American Psychiatrists Association 158-167, 201
Americans with Disabilities Act 40, 49, 56-58, 63-64, 78, 148, 201-203
Art about Impairments 17, 220-220
Art about Queerness 22, 113-116, 227-230
Ascanio Condivi 218, 223
Assisted Dying 94-95
Association of Gay and Lesbian Psychiatrists 164, 166-167
Autism (History) 123, 224
Autism (Modern) 123
Automatic Computing Engine 124
Barbara Gittings
Barbara Jordan **134**-140, 143-148, 150
Black Panthers 52
Blatt vs Cabela's Retail Inc 202
Bletchley Park 121-125, 127
Bobbie Lea Bennet **192**-194, 200-206, 208-212
Boston Center for Independent Living 77-78
Boston Self Help Center 77
Britney Spears 83, 91
Buggery Act 113
Byronmania 98, 106
Cambridge University 103-104, 119, 120-122
Camp Jened 42-44, 69

Index

Capitol Crawl 61
Catherine Odette 77
Centre for Independent Living, Berkley 46-48, 56
Chemical castration 126-127
Christine Jorgensen 196
Christopher Morcom 118-119
Christopher Street Liberation Day 31-32
Civilian Vocational Rehabilitation Act 149
Cold War 127
Connie Panzarino **66**-79
Conversion Therapy to Cure Disabled People 191
Conversion Therapy to cure Queer People (Electroconvulsive Therapy, Lobotomy, Deep Brain Stimulation, Aversion Therapy) 158, 187-191
Crime against Disabled people (sexual assault, physical assault, financial crimes, abuse, medical abuse) 14, 76, 84, 207
Crime against Queer people (sexual assault, physical assault, financial crimes, abuse, medical abuse) 14, 26, 28, 39, 76
Crip Camp 40-44, 52, 69
Deaf history 174, 220-221
Deprivation of Liberty 84-86
Diagnostic and Statistical Manual of Mental Disorders 155-158, 164-166, 201
Diego Rivera 16, 20-23
Disability Benefits 35, 70, 72, 192
Disability in Queer communities 12-15, 75, 87, 97
Disability Pride 78-79
Disability Pride Month 79
Disability Rights Education and Defense Fund 56-57, 64
Don Juan 111-113
Don Leon 113-116
Don't Ask Don't Tell 142
Dr Henry Anonymous 160-164, 166
Dr John Fryer **153**-155, 159-164, 166
Dr. Franklin E. Kameny 159-160, 163, 167
Drag Queen 24, 27, 29, 31
Dykes, Disability and Stuff 77
Ed Roberts 46
Edith Spurlock Sampson 136
Employment Equality (Sexual Orientation) Regulations (UK) 143

241

Employment Rights for Disabled People 72-75
Enigma 121-124
Entscheidungsproblem 119-120
Escuela Nacional Preparatoria (National Preparatory School) 16
European Court of Human Rights 86, 142
Evelyn Hooker 157
Experiments on Disabled People 207
Fair Housing Act 145, 201
Family of Affinity 92
Franz Mesmer 179-180, 182-183, 185
Fresh air as treatment/Countryside convalesence 100, 171-172, 174
Frida Kahlo **11**-17, 20-23
Fridamania 11, 23
Gay Liberation Front 31, 159
Gay Men's Health Crisis 33-24, 38
Gender Affirming Surgery (funding) 192, 199, 204-206, 208-210
Gender Affirming Surgery (history) 194-196, 197-200
Gender Identity Clinic, Galveston Texas 200-203
Gender Identity Clinics (US history) 194, 197-199
Gender Identity Foundation, Oklahoma 199
Gender Recognition Act (UK) 143
George W. Henry Foundation 155
German Scientific-Humanitarian Committee 141
Giogio Vasari 219-220, 223
Government Code and Cypher School 121
Government Communications Headquarters (GCHQ) 121, 127
Greenwich Village 27
Gross Indecency 126, 132
Guardianship (Historic) 81-83, 101
Guardianship (Modern) 81, 83-85, 87-88, 90-93
Harriet Martineau 19, **169**-186
Harry Benjamin International Gender Dysphoria Association/ World Professional Association for Transgender Health (WPATH) 199-200
HIV/AIDS 33-39, 62-63, 88, 167
Holy Roman Empire 226
Homelessness 28, 33, 39
Homeschooling 16-17, 68, 100, 172
Homosexuality as a Disease 13, 126, 130, 154-155, 157-160, 163-165, 188-191

Index

Homosexuality in the Ancient World 229-230
House Judiciary Committee (USA) 146
Hypnotism 186-188
Hysteria 179, 186-187
Illustrations on Political Economy 177
Indigenous/Native Populations 15, 21, 82
Institute for Sexual Science, Berlin 194
Institutionalisation (Children) 207-208
Institutionalisation (Disabled Adults) 65, 86-87, 90-91
Institutionalisation (Psychiatric) 27-28
International Work Group on Death, Dying, and Bereavement 155, 167
Intersectionality (Gender) 14, 17, 77, 176, 184, 187, 198, 202
Intersectionality (Race) 14, 82, 150
Intersectionality (Religion) 14, 17, 26, 171, 193
Issues with Diagnosing Historical Figures 99, 172, 216, 224
Issues with Outing Historical Figures 104, 175, 227
James Braid 186
James Lebrecht 44
James Pratt and John Smith 114
John Elliotson 185
John Hopkins University Gender Identity Clinic 198-199
John Kitto 220
John Wolfenden 130-132
Joseph Califano 51, 54
Judith Heumann 48
Karen Thompson 78, **80**-85, 87, 89-93, 96
Kinsey Report 156
Kitty Cone **40**-48, 54-57, 64-65
League of the Physically Handicapped 148
Leon Trotsky 22
Lord Byron (George Gordon Noel) **98**-114
Lovers of Lord Byron 98, 101, 103, 105, 107
Lyndon B. Johnson 138, 144, 146
Mad Jack Byron 99, 102-110
Maria Theresa Paradis 182
Marsha P. Johnson **24**-34, 38
Mary Shelley 111
Mattachine Foundation 141
Medicaid and 'Obamacare' 73, 203

243

Medicare 203-206, 208-209
Mesmerism (animal magnetism) 178-179, 181-183, 185-186
Michelangelo **213**-220, 223-228, 230-231
Mike Oliver 19
Milan Conference 174
Nancy Earl 140, 151
National Association for the Advancement of Colored People (NAACP) 64, 136
National Association for the Repeal of the Contagious Diseases Acts (UK) 184
National Council on Disability 58
National Employ the Physically Handicapped Week 149
National Free Sharon Kowalski Day 90
Offences Against the Persons Act (UK) 114
Office of Vocational Rehabilitation 71
Parenting 55, 194, 211
Patricia Peery 93
Paul McHugh 198
People United in Support of the Handicapped 71
Phrenology 185
Police and Crime Act (UK) 129
Polish codebreakers 122
Power of Attorney 89
Pride (event) 13, 75, 78
Princeton University 120-121
Psychopathia Sexualis (Sexual Psychopathy: A Clinical-Forensic Study) 187
Queen Victoria 115, 170, 184
Queer Bashing 28, 39
Queerphobia 13, 75-76, 85, 87, 127-128, 154, 165, 188-190
Renaissance 216-220, 223-231
Reproductive Control (forced sterilisation, forced contraceptives) 14, 83, 126
Richard Nixon 146-148, 161
Richard von Krafft-Ebing 187
Robert Galbraith Heath 188-189
Robert Wendland 96
Ron Kovic 72-75
Ronald Reagan 37, 58

Index

Royal Commission 182
Royal Perogative of Mercy 129
Royal Society Computing Machine Laboratory 125
Sara Karon 77
Segregation 135, 143
Sexual Offences Bill 132
Sharon Kowalski 78, **80**-85, 87, 89-93, 96
Sigmund Freud 154, 188
Sir Harold Gillies 195
Social Model of Disability 18-20, 37, 170-171
Sociology/Political Economy 169, 176, 184
Sodomy/Buggery (Crime) 110, 113-115, 126
Statement on the Articles of Impeachment 147
Stonewall Inn and other New York Gay Bars 27-28
Stonewall Riot 29-32, 159
Stormé DeLarverie 30
Street Transvestite Action Revolutionaries 31-32
Students for a Democratic Society 44
Suffragettes 181
Sylvia Rivera 31-32
Terri Schiavo 94
Texas Southern University 137
The Convention on the Rights of Persons with Disabilities (UN) 84
The Criminal Law Amendment Act (UK) 114
The Denver Principles 37
The National League of the Blind 148-149
The Rehabilitation Act 1973 and Section 504 (USA) 49-54, 56, 74, 96, 148, 150
The Society for Human Rights 141
The Transsexual Phenomenon 195-197
Tommaso dei Cavalieri 227-228
Transgender people and Discrimination 142-143, 201-203
Turing Machine 120, 124
Turing Test 125
UK Parliament (House of Commons) 101, 129, 132
UK Parliament (House of Lords) 86, 101, 105, 129, 132
Union of the Physically Impaired Against Segregation 19
US Government (Senate) 61, 139, 143
US Government (House of Representatives) 57-58, 64, 141, 150-151

US Supreme Court 57-58, 64, 141, 150-151
Vatican/Pope 217-220, 224-225
Watergate 134, 146-148
Wilfred Owen 221-222
Willowbrook State School 206-208
Wolfenden Report 130-132
World War 1 221-222
World War 2 117, 121-123, 130, 141-142, 149, 204, 206
Young Socialist Alliance 45